PHILADELPHIA
SPORTS
QUIZ

PHILADELPHIA SPORTS QUIZ

Brenda Alesii
&
Daniel Locche

A Citadel Press Book
Published by Carol Publishing Group

A Citadel Press Book
Published by Carol Publishing Group

Citadel Press is a registered trademark of Carol
Communications, Inc.

Editorial Offices: 600 Madison Avenue, New York, N.Y. 10022
Sales & Distribution Offices: 120 Enterprise Avenue, Secaucus,
    N.J. 07094
In Canada: Canadian Manda Group, P.O. Box 920, Station U,
    Toronto, Ontario M8Z 5P9

Queries regarding rights and permissions should be addressed to
Carol Publishing Group, 600 Madison Avenue, New York, N.Y. 10022

Carol Publishing Group books are available at special discounts
for bulk purchases, for sales promotions, fund-raising, or
educational purposes. Special editions can be created to specifications.
For details, contact Special Sales Department, Carol Publishing
Group, 120 Enterprise Avenue, Secaucus, N.J. 07094

Manufactured in the United States of America
10 9 8 7 6 5 4 3 2 1

Library of Congress Cataloging-in-Publication Data

Alesii, Brenda.
    Philadelphia sports quiz : Phillies, 76ers,
Flyers, Eagles / by Brenda Alesii and Daniel Locche.
        p. cm.
    "A Citadel Press book."
    ISBN 0-8065-1416-7
    1. Sports—Pennsylvania—Philadelphia—Miscellanea. I. Locche,
Dan. II. Title.
GV584.5.P46A44 1993
796'.09748'11—dc20   92-38084
                                                          CIP

Contents

Acknowledgments

Philadelphia Sports Quiz is the sixth in our line of sports trivia books. Preceding this edition are *New York Sports Quiz, Boston Sports Quiz, Chicago Sports Quiz, Los Angeles Sports Quiz* and *Baltimore–Washington Sports Quiz.* We are well on our way to producing a series of books detailing the sports facts and histories in selected cities throughout the United States and Canada.

Our goal for each book is simple. We attempt to provide an entertaining and informative compilation of particular cities' "big four" major league teams under one cover. Included in every edition are offbeat, fascinating, and intriguing aspects of pro sports, as well as a statistical chronicle of the franchises.

We derive great pleasure from writing the books because of our almost obsessive love of sports, our desire to travel, and the mutual emjoyment of working together. (Yes, we are a husband-and-wife team that actually relishes working together!) We've weathered some long nights and snowy roads in our effort to put together a product that we can be proud of, one that we hope will settle some arguments, start a few, and provide endless hours of enjoyment.

The friendships that developed from the production of our books are the greatest reward of all. Many thanks to the following for their assistance, guidance, and counsel:

Bob Salomon and Al Marill of Carol Publishing Group
Tom Hietz and the staff at the Baseball Hall of Fame
Wayne Patterson and the staff at the Basketball Hall of
Fame
Joe Horrigan, Pete Fierle, Sandy Self, and the staff at the
Football Hall of Fame
Phil Pritchart and the staff at the Hockey Hall of Fame
The Phillies, Flyers, Sixers, and Eagles
Our families and friends, who offer unwavering support and
tolerate us as our deadline approaches.

Photos included in this book were obtained from the
following sources:

Basketball: Hall of Fame, Springfield, Massachusetts
Baseball: National Baseball Library, Cooperstown, New
York
Football: Hall of Fame, Canton, Ohio, and NFL Properties
Hockey: Hall of Fame, Toronto, Ontario, Canada

Please note: While the Warriors and Athletics were noteworthy
teams with distinguished histories, we decided the passage of
time may have removed much of the detailed information on
those teams from the sports mind of the Philadelphia fan. On
that basis, we decided against including them in this edition.

Dedication

This book is dedicated to the memory of Anthony B. Locche, a man who deeply loved sports, and a man who was loved deeply by his family and the countless friends who had the privilege to make his acquaintance.

How to Use
Philadelphia Sports Quiz

Philadelphia Sports Quiz is divided into four chapters: the Phillies, 76ers, Flyers, and Eagles. Each section contains questions, answers, and "fast facts" pertaining to the particular team.

For your convenience, the question page always precedes the answer page; questions are grouped separately from their respective answers. (A "Q" represents a question, while an "A" indicates an answer.) Each chapter reflects the chronology of the team. It is divided into separate categories in the following manner: "Suits" denotes coaches, managers, and front-office personnel; "Uniforms" involves the players; "Setting the Standard" is about records; "FYI" is general information; "Glory Days" covers the playoffs and any postseason activity; and "Trades, Waives, and Acquisitions" are just that.

The questions are current as of February 1993.

As is generally recognized, Philadelphia is home to some of the most knowledgeable sports fans in the country. In compiling the hundreds of questions and answers, we may have overlooked some facts and figures. We ask your indulgence.

If you have a particular bit of information to add or would like to discuss the contents of *Philadelphia Sports Quiz*, we encourage you to contact us.

Philadelphia Phillies

PHILADELPHIA PHILLIES

Philadelphia Phillies—1980

THE SUITS

Q1 This Phillie manager had some notorious run-ins with umpires: He once climbed a 14-foot tower after he was thrown out of a game, and on another occasion managed the team by walkie-talkie from the parking lot after he was given the thumb. Name the feisty skipper.

Q2 What Phillie owner was barred from the game after it was discovered in 1943 that he was betting on his own team?

Q3 Identify the three native Philadelphians who have managed the team.

Q4 At age 30, he was the youngest Phillie manager in the modern era. Who was he?

Q5 What team did Alfred Reach and Colonel John Rogers purchase in 1883 and move to the City of Brotherly Love?

Q6 In 1894, this manager began a 10-year stint at the Phillie helm. He was a native of England, a star cricket player, and the skipper of the 1869 and '70 Cincinnati Reds. Who was he?

Q7 The Phillies were sold in 1909 to a group of investors headed by Horace Fogel, but the NL barred the new president from all league meetings. Why?

Q8 An outstanding defensive catcher during the first decade of the twentieth century, this Phillie was the first to use papier-mâché shin guards. He became the club's player-manager in 1910 and stayed at the Philadelphia helm for four seasons. Who was he?

Q9 This manager's tenure ended in 1920 and he later became a justice of the peace in California. Who was he?

PHILADELPHIA PHILLIES

A1   Frank Lucchesi

A2   William Cox

A3   Bill Shettsline (1898–1902)
          Jimmy Wilson (1934–38)
          Lee Elia (1987–88)

A4   Red Dooin (1910–14)

A5   The Worcester Brown Stockings of the National League

A6   Harry Wright

A7   Fogel was a sportswriter, and the league felt that the dual roles were a
          conflict of interest.

A8   Charles "Red" Dooin

A9   Gavvy Cravath

*** FAST FACTS ***

Phillie Jim Bunning set a league record with five 1–0 losses during the
1967 season.

Although he led in strikeouts (162) for the fourth straight year, Juan
Samuel in 1987 became the first player to rack up double figures in
homers, triples, doubles, and stolen bases in each of his first four years.

Jack "Lucky" Lohrke earned his nickname when he was called off the
Double A team bus fifteen minutes before departure to go up to a Triple
A club. The vehicle crashed into a ravine, killing eight players.

At 6'6½", Frank Sullivan of the Red Sox was the tallest pitcher in the AL.
In December 1960, he was dispatched to the Phillies for the National
League's tallest hurler, 6'8" Gene Conley.

Kent Tekulve did not play professional ball until the age of 22.

Q10 This former shortstop became the Phillies' manager for four unsuccessful seasons (1923–26). In 1927, he became the Yankees' assistant coach under Miller Huggins, and remained with the New York franchise until his retirement. Who was he?

Q11 After finishing at the bottom of the heap in 1927, this Phillie manager quit the big leagues and went to the Ivy Leagues, where he coached five years at Harvard. Who was he?

Q12 James Thompson Prothro, better known as "Doc," racked up a 138–320 record when he managed the club from 1939–41. How did he earn his nickname?

Q13 This Phillie managed the club for only two games in 1938 (going 0–2) but returned at the helm for all of the 1942 season (42–111). As a player in Philadelphia, he stole home six times, tying him for second on the club's all-time list. Name him.

Q14 The release of this Phillie manager during the 1943 season almost resulted in a players' strike because of the team's loyalty to him. Who inspired such a following?

Q15 Late in 1943, Robert R. M. Carpenter plunked down $400,000 and purchased the Phils from William Cox. At what company was Carpenter a vice president?

Q16 Before John Quinn took over the GM's reins in 1959, he earned his baseball stripes with another team that eventually relocated to another city. With what club did Quinn work?

Q17 Gene Mauch had a long stint as the Phils' skipper after he replaced this manager, who called it quits after the opening game of the 1960 season. Whom did Mauch supplant?

Q18 Gene Mauch was named NL Manager of the Year in 1962 (81–80). A year before, Mauch wasn't as fortunate as he suffered through a modern-day losing streak. How long did it last?

Q19 A Phillie scout for 27 years, he was also renowned for his work as basketball captain at St. Joe's and as an NBA referee and supervisor of officials. Who was this versatile sportsman?

Q20 When a rash of injuries struck the 1970 Phillies, this bullpen coach was reactivated to play catcher and responded with two game-winning ribbies. Who was he?

PHILADELPHIA PHILLIES

A10   Art Fletcher

A11   Stuffy McGinnis

A12   He was a dentist in the off-season.

A13   Hans Lobert

A14   Bucky Harris

A15   duPont

A16   The Boston/Milwaukee Braves

A17   Eddie Sawyer

A18   The streak went on for 23 consecutive losses.

A19   Jocko Collins

A20   Doc Edwards

*** FAST FACTS ***

As manager of the Phillies from 1919 to 1920, Gavvy Cravath was considered too easygoing for the job. After his managerial stint, Cravath became a justice of the peace in Laguna, California, but was dismissed from the position for being too lenient.

In the new age of technology, the Phillies cut corners to win. In a September 17 game, a wire was found by the Reds' third base coach to run from the coaching box to the outfield locker room so the club could steal the opposing catcher's signs and relay them to the Phils' coach. The year: 1900!

Q21 Who piloted the Phils when the club beat Montreal, 2–1, in the final game at Connie Mack and in the first game at Veterans Stadium when the team whitewashed Chicago, 2–0?

Q22 A Purple Heart recipient from his service at the Battle of the Bulge, this Buffalo native spent 31 years in the Dodger organization and was named Phils' manager in late 1972. Who was he?

Q23 How old was Ruly Carpenter when he was named president of the team in 1972?

Q24 For what university was Ruly Carpenter the captain of the baseball team and a two-way end on the undefeated football club?

Q25 When Dallas Green guided the Phils to the world championship in 1980, he became only the third ML pitcher to do so. Who were his two predecessors in that category?

Q26 Dallas Green recorded all of his major league decisions as a pitcher with the Phillies, even though he played for three teams during his playing career. For what other two clubs did Green pitch?

Q27 Baseball is in Bill Giles's blood—his father was the GM of the Cincinnati Reds, and NL president from 1951–69. Who was he?

Q28 Besides the Phillies, with what ML teams did Pat Corrales play?

Q29 With what team did Pat Corrales make his big league debut in 1964?

Q30 Under what ex-Phillie skipper did Pat Corrales spend three years as a coach for the Texas Rangers?

Q31 In what university's Hall of Fame is Paul Owens an inductee?

Q32 What two managers did Paul Owens replace on separate occasions before being named manager in 1984?

Q33 His college coach said halfback Lee Elia was the "best pure athlete I've ever seen." At what school did Elia gain gridiron glory?

Q34 Lee Elia was a dugout assistant to the man he would eventually replace as the team's manager. From whom did Elia take over on June 18, 1987?

Q35 Although he never played in the majors, this team drafted infielder Nick Leyva in June 1975. Which club plucked the California native in the 24th round?

PHILADELPHIA PHILLIES

A21   Frank Lucchesi

A22   Danny Ozark

A23   32 years old

A24   Yale

A25   Eddie Dyer (1946–St. Louis Cardinals)
Bob Lemon (1978–New York Yankees)

A26   Washington Senators (1965: 6 games, 14.1 innings pitched)
New York Mets (1966: 4 games, 5 innings pitched)

A27   Warren Giles

A28   Cards
Reds
Padres

A29   Phillies

A30   Frank Lucchesi

A31   St. Bonaventure's (1977)

A32   Frank Lucchesi (July 10, 1972: 33–47)
Pat Corrales (July 18, 1983: 47–30)

A33   University of Delaware

A34   John Felske

A35   St. Louis Cardinals

THE SUITS

Q36   What position did Jim Fregosi hold with the Phils before he was elevated to manager in 1991?

Q37   Jim Fregosi was acquired by the Angels in the 1960 expansion draft; he played on the Left Coast from 1961–71. From what team did the Angels take Fregosi in that draft?

Q38   Before taking the Phillie helm, Jim Fregosi had big league experience with American League clubs. Identify the teams Fregosi managed in the late seventies and eighties.

Q39   Name the club that allowed player Jim Fregosi to leave in mid-season so that he could accept a major league managerial position.

THE UNIFORMS

Q1   Name the onetime Phillie who is the only major league player to be a teammate of both Hank Aaron and Japanese home-run king Sadaharu Oh.

Q2   What Phillie was a onetime bodyguard for singer Tina Turner?

Q3   Who was the first NL catcher to wear glasses?

Q4   "Versatile" was an apt description for this Phillie: He played football with Knute Rockne, was a star hurdler and sprinter, and studied architecture at Notre Dame. Who was this well-rounded athlete?

Q5   Name the former Phillie who bragged about urinating in the outfield of every major league park.

Q6   Name the quartet of players whose numbers have been retired by the Phils.

Q7   Who is the only Phil to wear uniform number 0?

Q8   The Phillies opened the twentieth century with a third-place finish in the 1900 season. Who was the leading hitter for the club that year?

Q9   Shortstop Arthur Irwin (1886–89, 1894) designed and patented this piece of baseball equipment and was the first player to wear it on the diamond. What did Irwin popularize?

PHILADELPHIA PHILLIES

A36   Fregosi was a minor league pitching instructor/special assignments manager.

A37   Boston Red Sox

A38   California Angels (1978–81)
Chicago White Sox (1986–88)

A39   Pittsburgh Pirates (The Pirates released Fregosi on June 1, 1978.)

———————————— · ————————————

A1   Davey Johnson

A2   Lance Parrish

A3   Stan Lopata

A4   Cy Williams

A5   Rick Bosetti

A6   Mike Schmidt—Number 20 (1990)
Steve Carlton—Number 32 (1989)
Richie Ashburn—Number 1 (1979)
Robin Roberts—Number 36 (1962)

A7   Al Oliver

A8   Elmer Flick (.378)

A9   A baseball glove

Q10   Who were the first two Phillies to be named to the inaugural All-Star Game, held in 1933?

Q11   Although he became famous as an outfielder, Ed Delahanty played another position when he signed with the Phils in 1888. Where did he initially play?

Q12   Ed Delahanty defected to another league in 1890 before returning to the Phils the next year. Where did Big Ed play for that one season?

Q13   In what tragic and bizarre manner did Ed Delahanty die in 1903?

Q14   Lou Chiozza of the Phillies was the first man in the history of baseball to do something, in a game played against the Reds on May 24, 1935. How did Chiozza distinguish himself?

Q15   Who was the first Phil outfielder to win a Gold Glove?

Q16   What Phillie won the first Rookie of the Year Award distributed by *The Sporting News*?

Q17   Acknowledged as Philly's first baseball star, this player had a 30–9 mark on the mound in 1886 and, a year later, hit .337. Two years later, he contracted typhoid fever and died at age 25. Who was this early-day superstar?

Q18   When the Phillies debuted in 1883, the team carried a two-man pitching staff. Name the marathon man who racked up a 12–48 record in that first campaign.

Q19   This favorite son played for the Phillies from 1884–97 and made a name for himself as a left-handed catcher. Who was he?

Q20   In 1888, the Phils added a player known as "Kid," who later gained notoriety as the manager of the 1919 White Sox, the team that threw the World Series. Who was he?

Q21   Name the Phillie who led the National League in home runs in 1900.

Q22   What trio of Hall of Famers played in the Philadelphia outfield from 1891–95?

Q23   Name the Phillie who was the youngest regular major league player of the twentieth century.

PHILADELPHIA PHILLIES

A10   Dick Bartell
Chuck Klein
(Both were starters.)

A11   Second base

A12   The Players' League

A13   He fell off the International Bridge near Niagara Falls and was swept over the falls to his death. (Delahanty was 35 years old.)

A14   He was the first man to bat in a major league night game. (He led off for the Phils in Cincinnati.)

A15   Garry Maddox (1975)

A16   Del Ennis (1946)

A17   Charlie Ferguson

A18   John Coleman

A19   Jack Clements

A20   William Gleason

A21   Herman Long (12 homers)

A22   Billy Hamilton
Sam Thompson
Ed Delahanty

A23   Johnny Lush (1904: 18 years old)

Q24 When the American League was established in 1901, a number of Phillies jumped to the new organization. Who was the first Philadelphia player to return to his former team?

Q25 From 1888 through 1901, this Hall of Famer was one of Philadelphia's first power hitters. He led the league in RBIs three times (1893, '96, '99), homers once (1893), and batting average once (1899). He also had four brothers who played in the major leagues. Name him.

Q26 After this Phillie left the club, he eventually wound up in Cleveland. Following the 1907 season, the Detroit Tigers offered to swap 21-year-old Ty Cobb for the 31-year-old outfielder. Who is this Hall of Famer?

Q27 This player was the Phillies' left fielder from 1904 until 1914. When he was bypassed as player-manager in 1915, he asked to be traded. Who was he?

Q28 A versatile deadball-era player, this Phillie once knocked out an umpire after he was thrown out of a 1911 game. Who was this hot-tempered player?

Q29 Thanks to his feat of defeating the contending Giants three times in five days, this Pennsylvania native earned a $50 bonus and the moniker "The Giant Killer." Who was he?

Q30 What was Grover Cleveland Alexander's nickname?

Q31 From what New York State League club did the Phillies buy Grover Cleveland Alexander for the whopping fee of $1,000 in 1910?

Q32 In what categories did Grover Alexander lead the National League in his rookie season?
(A) Wins
(B) Complete Games
(C) Innings Pitched
(D) Shutouts
(E) All of the Above

Q33 For what three major league teams did Grover Cleveland Alexander play?

Q34 Alexander the Great's favorite catcher was nicknamed "Reindeer." The battery mates were traded from the Phils in a 1917 package. Who was Alexander's pal?

Q35 After the Phils sent Alexander to the Cubs, the team had several straight second-division finishes. Over how many seasons did that skein extend?

PHILADELPHIA PHILLIES

A24   Bill Duggleby (Frosty Bill played only two games for the crosstown rivals, the Athletics, before returning to the Phillies.)

A25   Ed Delahanty

A26   Elmer Flick

A27   Sherry Magee (He was dealt to the Braves.)

A28   Sherry Magee

A29   Harry Covelski

A30   "Pete"

A31   Syracuse

A32   (E)—Wins: 28
         Complete Games: 31
         Innings Pitched: 367
         Shutouts: 7 (including 4 consecutive)

A33   Phillies (1911–17)
         Chicago Cubs (1917–25)
         St. Louis Cardinals (1926–30)

A34   BIll Killefer

A35   14

*** FAST FACTS ***

Hall of Famer "Big Ed" Delahanty made a big splash on and off the field. While playing ball, he led the majors in batting average twice, RBIs three times, and once for homers. His life ended in 1903 when he was ejected from a train for being drunk and disorderly, fell off a bridge, and was swept to his death over Niagara Falls.

Considered one of the most outdated parks in the majors when it was abandoned in 1938, the Baker Bowl was the scene of a tragic accident during a 1903 doubleheader. On August 8, the third base stands collapsed, killing 12 fans. It was also famous because no ball ever cleared the 35-foot wall of the center-field clubhouse.

Q36 Alexander registered 373 wins in his illustrious career, equaling the National League record for victories. Whose mark did he equal?

Q37 Grover Alexander ran up 30 wins in 1917. Who would be the next Phillie pitcher to become a 20-game winner?

Q38 How many no-hitters did Alex hurl in his brilliant major league career?

Q39 Who portrayed Grover Alexander in the movie *The Winning Team*?

Q40 How old was rookie Gavvy Cravath when he debuted with the Phils in 1912?

Q41 Maybe it was because his career was short-lived, or the fact that he played during the "deadball" era, but Happy Finneran turned to an odd career after his two seasons in major league ball. In what job did he bury himself after baseball?

Q42 This right-handed pitcher was 14–11 in Philly's 1915 pennant-winning season. The following year, he defeated Philadelphia in both games of a doubleheader for Chicago. After retiring from pro ball in 1920, he became a syndicated sports cartoonist. Name this former Phillie.

Q43 What was Hall of Famer Dave Bancroft's nickname?

Q44 Who is the only major leaguer to lose his life in World War I?

Q45 Because this Phillie wielded such a hot bat over the course of his career, opposing managers implemented a fielding change that required the outfield to move entirely to the right side of the field. For what player was this done?

Q46 In the majors for four and a half seasons prior to coming to the Phillies in 1919, this infielder hit a career-high .288 in 1920. Immediately after the season, he was banned from baseball by Commissioner Kenesaw Mountain Landis for accepting gifts from gamblers. Who was he?

Q47 This Phillie pitcher so enraged Casey Stengel when he hurled a fastball by his ear in a 1923 game that Stengel flung his bat at him and had to be removed from the field by Philadelphia police. Who set Casey off?

Q48 What rule was instituted by major league baseball in 1925 because of Phillie pitcher Bill Hubbell?

PHILADELPHIA PHILLIES

A36   Christy Mathewson's

A37   Robin Roberts (1950: 20–11)

A38   None

A39   Ronald Reagan (Doris Day played his wife.)

A40   31 years old

A41   He became a funeral director.

A42   Al Demaree

A43   "Beauty"

A44   Eddie Grant (Phillies: 1907–1910)

A45   Cy Williams (The defensive move was called the "Williams shift.")

A46   Gene Paulette

A47   Lefty Weinert

A48   The rule required all pitches to be thrown to the catcher. (Twice during the season, Hubbell intentionally walked a batter by throwing four pitches to the first baseman.)

*** FAST FACTS ***

In 1909, Grover Cleveland Alexander was playing for Galesburg, Ill., of the Central Association. In an attempt to break up a double play, he took the shortstop's relay in the head, was unconscious for two days, and awoke with double vision. Still disoriented, he was dispatched to Indianapolis of the American Association. After his first pitch at practice broke three of the manager's ribs, he was immediately sent home and his contract was sold to the Syracuse Chiefs. The following year, he won 29 games for the Chiefs, including 15 shutouts.

THE UNIFORMS

Q49 The Phils' starting shortstop for six seasons, this player was asked to throw a game against the Giants so the New York team could secure the 1924 pennant. He refused, reported the bribe, and the crooked players were suspended for life. Who was this scrupulous Phillie?

Q50 How many separate tenures did Chuck Klein have with the Phillies?

Q51 Though Chuck Klein won the Triple Crown in 1933 (28 HR, 120 RBIs, .368 avg.), he was not selected as the league's MVP. Who won the honor that year?

Q52 When this former Phillie infielder became the manager of the White Sox in 1932, he pioneered the use of film to analyze his players. He later promoted the game through movies as director of promotions for both the AL and NL. Name him.

Q53 This lefty came into the league with the Phillies in 1928. In four of his first five major league seasons, he batted over .300, including a .339 season with 24 homers and a league-leading 143 RBIs. Name him.

Q54 Name the 1929 starting catcher for the Phillies who was killed by an automobile in the off-season.

Q55 Name the Phillie infielder who, after complaining of a stomachache and undergoing an operation, died during the 1933 season.

Q56 Switch-hitter Buzz Arlett of the Phillies had a .341 average and 432 dingers in his brilliant minor league career. Yet, his major league career lasted just one season. How old was Arlett when he reached "the Show"?

Q57 This pitcher debuted in the majors with a 1–0 shutout of the Reds on September 17, 1935. His career would span four seasons, all with the Phillies, and he would win only three more games. Name him.

Q58 Called "Losing Pitcher" because the initials "LP" often followed his name in the box scores, this early-day Phillie was the first big leaguer drafted by the army. Who was he?

Q59 Probably best known as a manager, this player led the NL in stolen bases as a Phillie rookie in 1941. Name him.

Q60 How did wartime slugger Elvin "Buster" Adams get his nickname?

Q61 What Hall of Famer finished his stellar career with the Phils a short time after World War II and ended up pitching nine games in 1945?

PHILADELPHIA PHILLIES

A49 Heinie Sand

A50 Three (1928–33; 1936–39; 1940–44)

A51 Carl Hubbell

A52 Lew Fonseca

A53 Don Hurst

A54 Walt Lerian

A55 Mickey Finn

A56 32 years old (In 1984, Arlett was voted the outstanding player in minor league baseball history by the Society for American Baseball Research.)

A57 Hal Kelleher

A58 Hugh Mulcahy

A59 Danny Murtaugh

A60 Adams resembled Buster Brown, the shoe company's logo.

A61 Jimmie Foxx

*** FAST FACTS ***

The hosts of the 1914 World Series, Boston and Philadelphia, also held the 1915 Series, though with different clubs. In 1914, the Braves played the Athletics, and the Phillies met the Red Sox the following season. Unfortunately, Philadelphia was on the losing end both seasons.

Dick Farrell made his major league debut as a starter in 1956 and lost his first game. His next 258 appearances came in relief.

Richie makes an impression on Alice: On August 17, 1957, Phillie fan Alice Roth was hit with a foul ball off the bat of Richie Ashburn. She suffered a broken nose. During the same at-bat, Ashburn struck Roth again...as she lay on a stretcher.

Q62 Name the eldest of three baseball siblings who wore a Phillie uniform for two seasons (1945 and '46) and who belted a club-record four grand slams.

Q63 From what local high school did Del Ennis hail?

Q64 This Phillie first baseman was hitting better than .300 in mid-1949 when he was shot and nearly killed by a young woman in a Chicago hotel. That incident became the inspiration for *The Natural*. What player was caught in the middle of that bizarre situation?

Q65 Name the pitcher who in 1950 led the league in wins (16) and saves (22), set a major league record (since surpassed) with 74 appearances, and led the Phillies to the pennant.

Q66 Dubbed the ultimate singles hitter, this player hit over .300 nine times, won two batting titles, led the National League four times in walks, and batted .300 in his last season. Name this onetime Phillie.

Q67 What honor did Richie Ashburn walk away with after the 1948 season?

Q68 Labeled the greatest Phillie pitcher since Grover Alexander, this man on the mound was a baseball and basketball star at Michigan State. Who was this hurler?

Q69 Hall of Fame resident Robin Roberts brought his skills to the collegiate level when he took the head coaching position at a Southern school. Where did he ply his trade?

Q70 An All-Star and MVP in 1950, this Syracuse product developed a palmball and hooked on with the Phillies at the age of 32. Who was this late bloomer?

Q71 Willie Jones, a Phillie fixture at third base for a decade (1949–58), had a memorable nickname. What was it?

Q72 Who were the core players on the 1950 Philadelphia Whiz Kids?

Q73 Debuting at age 19 with the Phillies, he was given $100,000 to sign with the club. Over six disappointing seasons, the infielder batted only .217 and had 14 homers. Name him.

Q74 Though the Phillies gave up five players to acquire him in 1957, this shortstop lasted only two seasons in the City of Brotherly Love before being traded to the Tigers. In his eight-year career, he was traded five times. Who is this well-traveled Cuban?

PHILADELPHIA PHILLIES

A62   Vincent DiMaggio

A63   Olney High

A64   Eddie Waitkus (He returned to the Phils in 1950 and batted .284.)

A65   Jim Konstanty

A66   Richie Ashburn

A67   Rookie of the Year

A68   Robin Roberts

A69   University of South Florida (Tampa)

A70   Jim Konstanty

A71   "Puddin' Head"

A72   Richie Ashburn
           Granny Hammer
           Robin Roberts
           Jim Konstanty
           Del Ennis
           Curt Simmons

A73   Ted Kazanski

A74   Humberto "Chico" Fernandez

THE UNIFORMS

Q75 Chuck Essegian, a onetime Phillie, is one of two players to swat two pinch-hit homers in a World Series (Essegian did it in 1959 while playing for the Dodgers). Who is the only other player to do so?

Q76 Warren Hacker pursued his father's dream and became a baseball pitcher. His career spanned 12 seasons, including one and a half years with Philly. What was Hacker's true aspiration?

Q77 Only five men since 1959 have been player-managers in the major leagues. Name the two onetime Phillies who are included in this category.

Q78 What was Sparky Anderson's given name?

Q79 What position did Sparky Anderson play with the Phillies?

Q80 How long was Sparky Anderson's big league playing career?

Q81 After he was brought up to the Phils in 1960, this right-hander picked off his first three base runners: Curt Flood and Bill White of the Cards, then the Giants' Jim Marshall in his next appearance. Name the hurler.

Q82 The starting 1960 catcher, this Phil was a heavyweight champ and the winner of the Chicago Invitational Boxing Cup. Name him.

Q83 After playing three seasons for the Phillies, this pitcher was traded to the Cubs in 1960 and tossed a no-hitter against St. Louis in his first start for Chicago. He is the only pitcher to ever achieve that feat. Name him.

Q84 With the Phillies from 1960–68, this player was the first regular center fielder ever to field 1.000. Who achieved that impressive feat?

Q85 When this infielder arrived in Philadelphia in 1960, manager Eddie Sawyer called him "the worst player I ever saw." After one season, 32 hits, 2 homers, and a .227 average, he was sold to the Cubs. Name him.

Q86 What screwballer saved 59 games for the Phillies from 1961–65 and led the league with a dozen relief wins in 1962?

Q87 Dick Allen started his major league career as a third baseman, but four years later he was switched to playing first base and the outfield. What precipitated the change of positions?

Q88 After a suspension and fine for unbecoming off-the-field behavior, Dick Allen was traded to St. Louis at the end of the 1969 season. Curt Flood was to report to Philly in the deal, but he challenged the reserve clause and refused to report to his new club. Who did the Cards substitute for Flood?

PHILADELPHIA PHILLIES

A75   Bernie Carbo (1975: for the Red Sox)

A76   He wanted to become a coal miner like his father.

A77   Solly Hemus (St. Louis: 1959)
Pete Rose (Cincinnati: 1984–86)

A78   George Lee Anderson

A79   Second base

A80   One year (1959)

A81   Art Mahaffey

A82   Clay Dalrymple

A83   Don Cardwell

A84   Tony Gonzalez

A85   Ted Lepcio

A86   Jack Baldschun

A87   Allen's throwing ability was hampered after he severely cut his hand while pushing a stalled car.

A88   Willie Montanez

*** FAST FACTS ***

The Maddux brothers—Greg of Chicago and Mike of the Phillies—made big league history when they faced each other in a September 1986 game. Greg emerged victorious in the first match of rookie brothers in the majors.

In a magnanimous gesture, the Phillies flew Wes Chamberlain's mother in from Chicago to see her son play on Mother's Day, 1992. Immediately after the game, the club sent the outfielder down to the minors.

THE UNIFORMS

Q89 The well-traveled Dick Allen went from the Phillies to the Cardinals to the Dodgers to the White Sox to the Phillies and finally to the A's with a brief stopover in Atlanta in between. What player was traded twice for Allen within a six-month period?

Q90 Who were the last two brothers to play for the Phillies at the same time?

Q91 Which Phillie player's fielding was so inept he was referred to as "Dr. Strangeglove"?

Q92 On June 21, 1964, Jim Bunning became the first NLer to toss a perfect game in the twentieth century. Against what club did he throw perfection?

Q93 After hanging up his cleats for good, Jim Bunning took the political mound and ran unsuccessfully for governor. In what state did this athlete turn pol?

Q94 Vic Power and Rick Wise both sported the highest uniform number worn by a Phillie player. What digit did they each don?

Q95 This Phil was the first player in the bigs to reach 100 hits in 1965. Who hit the century mark for the first time that season?

Q96 Bob Uecker had a short stint in Philadelphia after he was acquired in a 1965 multiplayer deal. In what movie did the funnyman portray himself as a Cleveland Indian broadcaster?

Q97 How many pennant-winning teams did Ferguson Jenkins pitch for during his career?

Q98 Gary Wagner, an ace in the 1965 Phillie bullpen, held a master's degree in a subject not usually associated with baseball. What was Wagner's area of expertise?

Q99 National League chief Bill White played for the Phils from 1966–68. What position did the All-Star play?

Q100 Shortstop Dick Groat, who never played minor league ball, ended his 14-year professional career with the Phillies. At what school was he an All-American basketball player?

Q101 Name the 1953 AL Rookie of the Year who finished his career with the Phillies in 1966.

Q102 This player hit the first National League grand slam in a World Series while playing for the Giants in 1962. Five years later, he made a brief stop in Philadelphia and played in 31 games. Who is this infielder?

PHILADELPHIA PHILLIES

A89   Jim Essian (The Phillies sent Essian to Atlanta as part of the deal for Allen, and the Braves then forwarded Essian to Chicago to complete their deal in Atlanta's acquisition of Allen.)

A90   Dennis and Dave Bennett (1964)

A91   Dick Stuart

A92   New York Mets (6–0)

A93   Kentucky (He was elected to the House of Representatives in 1986.)

A94   Number 62

A95   Richie Allen (187 hits for the year)

A96   *Major League*

A97   None

A98   Zoology

A99   First base

A100   Duke

A101   Harvey Kuenn (Kuenn was with the Tigers when he won the award.)

A102   Chuck "Iron Hands" Hiller

Q103   Though this Phillie tied a major league record for strikeouts by a rookie, he was selected to the Topps Rookie All-Star Team. Name him.

Q104   To whom was Tim McCarver referring when he said, "They're going to bury us sixty feet, six inches apart"?

Q105   What was unusual about Tim McCarver's six-game stint with the Phillies in 1980?

Q106   Name the Phillie who edged out Carl Yastrzemski for the 1970 AL batting race.

Q107   Dick Selma hailed from the same high school as Tom Seaver, Jim Maloney, and Dick Ellsworth. What is their alma mater?

Q108   Identify the former Phil who toured with Eddie Feigner's "King and His Court" four-man softball team in the late 1970s.

Q109   The same year he was acquired in a trade, this pitcher led the NL with nine relief wins. The greatest accomplishment of his career was holding Hank Aaron hitless in 22 appearances against him. Name this two-time Phillie.

Q110   Larry Bowa set a record during the 1972 season for the fewest errors by a shortstop. How many did he commit that year?

Q111   Only one major leaguer has played more games at the shortstop position than Larry Bowa. Name him.

Q112   For what major league club did Larry Bowa have a short-lived stint as manager in 1988?

Q113   True or false—Steve Carlton is the only pitcher to ever capture four Cy Young Awards.

Q114   Steve Carlton was acquired from the Cardinals in one of the best trades ever made by the Phillies. Who did Philadelphia give up in the deal?

Q115   Who is the only southpaw to register more lifetime wins than Steve Carlton?

Q116   Steve Carlton set a major league record (since broken) when he struck out 19 batters in a game, while pitching for St. Louis. Ironically, he lost the game, 4–3. Against what team did he accomplish this?

Q117   In the game cited above, who hit two home runs, accounting for all four RBIs, and cost Steve Carlton the victory?

PHILADELPHIA PHILLIES

A103   Larry Hisle

A104   Steve Carlton

A105   By playing with the Phils in 1980, McCarver became a four-decade player. (He started his career in 1959 by playing eight games with the Cards.)

A106   Alex Johnson (.3289 to .3286)

A107   Fresno High

A108   John Bateman

A109   Joe Hoerner

A110   Nine

A111   Luis Aparicio

A112   San Diego Padres (After a 16–30 start, Bowa was let go.)

A113   True (1972, 1977, 1980, and 1982)

A114   Rick Wise

A115   Warren Spahn (Spahn had 363 wins to Carlton's 329.)

A116   New York Mets

A117   Ron Swoboda

THE UNIFORMS

Q118 What publication named Steve Carlton left-handed pitcher of the decade (1970s)?

Q119 Though Bob Boone was the club's regular catcher, this 1976 acquisition stepped behind the plate when Steve Carlton took the mound. He played with Lefty at St. Louis, and helped his friend and former Cardinal battery mate to regain his old form. Name him.

Q120 Between 1972 and 1983, Steve Carlton was deemed the Phillie ace, but age (38), a loss of speed, and an inability to win his starts eventually forced him to a secondary position in the rotation. Who replaced him as the club's ace pitcher?

Q121 The Phillies asked 41-year-old Steve Carlton to retire in 1986, but Lefty pursued his major league career for two more seasons. How many clubs did he join after he left Philly?

Q122 At Stanford, this Phil was a pitcher-third baseman, but he later switched to catcher. His father, a star infielder in the 1950s, had moved from backstop to the infield. Who did not quite follow in his dad's footsteps?

Q123 For what team was Bob Boone's father, Ray, an All-Star third baseman?

Q124 Bob Boone did not secure the 1976 position of starting catcher until the original starter broke a collarbone in the season opener. Whose bad luck was Boone's good fortune?

Q125 Who replaced Bob Boone after the Phils traded the veteran backstop to the Angels in 1981?

Q126 The number one selection by the Phils in the 1972 draft, this hurler broke his collarbone in a charity bicycle tour. Who was he?

Q127 A unanimous choice for MVP honors, Mike Schmidt had an extraordinary 1980 season. What was his slugging average in that memorable campaign?

Q128 How long did Mike Schmidt toil in the minors before he was called up to the Show in 1972?

Q129 Whom did Mike Schmidt replace as the regular third baseman in 1973?

Q130 Identify the Astro who edged out sophomore Mike Schmidt for the 1974 Gold Glove Award.

PHILADELPHIA PHILLIES

A118 *Baseball Magazine*

A119 Tim McCarver

A120 John Denny

A121 Four (San Francisco Giants
          Chicago White Sox
          Cleveland Indians
          Minnesota Twins)

A122 Bob Boone

A123 The Detroit Tigers

A124 Johnny Oates's

A125 Keith Moreland

A126 Larry Christenson

A127 .624

A128 Two seasons

A129 Don Money (who was traded to the Brewers)

A130 Doug Rader

Q131   Mike Schmidt averaged 150 K's over the first four seasons of his career. What moniker did teammate Willie Montanez give Schmidt to indicate his problems at the plate?

Q132   In 1985 the Phillies moved Mike Schmidt from third to first base. Who replaced him for a brief time at the hot corner?

Q133   Who was announced as the starter at third base when Mike Schmidt retired during the 1989 season?

Q134   For what two clubs did Jim Lonborg play before coming to the Phillies in 1973?

Q135   Of Jim Lonborg's three career homers, one was a grand slam, on June 29, 1974. Against what club did he clear the bags for four runs?

Q136   Expectations were high when this much-touted player was chosen by the Phillies in the first round of the 1973 draft. Although he played every position except pitcher and catcher, he never lived up to reviews. Name him.

Q137   Before joining the Phillies in 1975 (for nine games), this player alternated in center field with an aging Willie Mays on the 1973 Mets. Who spelled the Say Hey Kid in his final season?

Q138   "Two-thirds of the earth is covered by water, the other one-third by this player." Who paid this compliment to Garry Maddox?

Q139   After Garry Maddox was traded to the Phillies in 1975, he snared eight straight Gold Gloves. Only two other players won more in the outfield. Name them.

Q140   Catcher Johnny Oates suffered a broken collarbone in the 1976 season opener due to a home plate collision in the ninth inning. Who caused the injury?

Q141   Before Bo Jackson and Deion Sanders, this Philly right-hander, who starred with the club during the seventies, played forward for the Detroit Pistons from 1965–67. (Due to a stipulation in his contract, he quit basketball for a full-time baseball career.) Name this versatile athlete.

Q142   How did Frank Edwin McGraw, better known as "Tug," earn his nickname?

Q143   What Phillie threesome made up the all-.300 outfield of 1976?

Q144   Besides the Phillies, with what major league teams did Bake McBride play?

PHILADELPHIA PHILLIES

A131   "A-choo"

A132   Rick Schu

A133   Chris James (A month later, James was traded from the Phillies.)

A134   Boston Red Sox (1965–1971)
Milwaukee Brewers (1972)

A135   Montreal Expos

A136   Alan Banister

A137   Don Hahn

A138   Phillie broadcaster Ralph Kiner

A139   Willie Mays (1957–68)
Roberto Clemente (1961–72)

A140   Pirate Dave Parker (Parker was called safe at home when Oates dropped the ball following the collision. The score forced the game into extra innings, and Pittsburgh went on to win the game.)

A141   Ron Reed

A142   He was given the moniker by his mother because he used to tug when she breast-fed him.

A143   Garry Maddox (.330)
Greg Luzinski (.304)
Jay Johnstone (.318)

A144   St. Louis Cardinals
Cleveland Indians

THE UNIFORMS

Q145   What is Bake McBride's real name?

Q146   In what category did Bake McBride lead all NL outfielders during the 1978 season?

Q147   With what professional baseball team was Davey Johnson a member immediately prior to joining the Phillies in 1977?

Q148   In 1973, Davey Johnson played for Atlanta and belted 43 home runs. That season, the Braves set a major league record by having three players who hit 40 or more dingers. Who accompanied Johnson in achieving that record?

Q149   The Phillies almost lost Richie Hebner to another professional sports club. Who was bidding for his services?

Q150   What was Richie Hebner's off-season job during the early years of his career?

Q151   Name the four Phils who won Gold Gloves in 1978.

Q152   What is Bud Harrelson's given name?

Q153   After 13 years with the Mets, Bud Harrelson was released following the 1977 season. Midway through the 1978 season, the Phillies picked up the infielder to help in their pennant-winning drive. What was Harrelson doing when Philadelphia signed up the free agent?

Q154   Shortly after being traded by Philadelphia in 1978, this left-hander ended Pete Rose's 44-game hit streak with a memorable strikeout. Who is this former Phillie?

Q155   When Pete Rose signed with the Phils on December 5, 1978, how long was his guaranteed contract for?

Q156   This Phillie led all NL pitchers in 1978 with three homers. Two of those dingers came in a critical September 30 game against the Pirates, helping the club to take the pennant. Name him.

Q157   Name the relief ace who led the Phils in saves with 16 in 1979.

Q158   This player, who was with the club in 1973 and '74, resurfaced as a free agent with the Phils in 1979 after stints with New York and Montreal. Name this well-traveled athlete.

PHILADELPHIA PHILLIES

A145   Arnold Ray

A146   Fielding

A147   Yomiuri Giants (of Japanese baseball)

A148   Hank Aaron (40)
Darrell Evans (41)

A149   Boston Bruins

A150   He was a grave digger at a cemetery run by his father.

A151   Bob Boone
Larry Bowa
Garry Maddox
Mike Schmidt

A152   Derrel McKinley

A153   He was playing professional softball.

A154   Gene Garber

A155   Four years

A156   Randy Lerch

A157   Tug McGraw

A158   Del Unser

Q39. Who portrayed Grover Alexander in the movie *The Winning Team?*

PHILADELPHIA PHILLIES

Q93. After hanging up his cleats for good, Jim Bunning took the political mound and ran unsuccessfully for governor. In what state did this athlete turn pol?

Q127. A unanimous choice for MVP honors, Mike Schmidt had an extraordinary 1980 season. What was his slugging average in that memorable campaign?

PHILADELPHIA PHILLIES

Q23. In what year was Shibe Park renamed Connie Mack Stadium?

Q159 This player, who was reacquired in a 1979 blockbuster deal, was originally signed by the Phils as a catcher in 1968 and broke into pro ball under Dallas Green at Huron. Name him.

Q160 How old was "Charlie Hustle" (Pete Rose) when he inked a free agent deal with the Phils for the 1979 season?

Q161 Who did Pete Rose replace as the Phillies' regular first baseman when he arrived in 1979?

Q162 Dick Ruthven's wife's twin sister was married to a former Phillie player. Who was her husband?

Q163 With what club did Sparky Lyle break into the majors?

Q164 How many games did Sparky Lyle start in his major league career?

Q165 How many at-bats did Ryne Sandberg have in a Phillie uniform?

Q166 A six-year veteran of the New Jersey National Guard, this outfielder almost quit baseball in 1975 to pursue a career as a blackjack dealer in Las Vegas. Name him.

Q167 With what team did Joe Morgan break into the majors in 1965, the year he won NL Rookie of the Year honors?

Q168 Who was named MVP of the 1979 U.S.–Japan College World Series?

Q169 Three onetime "Big Red Machine" stars were on the Phils' 1983 roster. Identify the trio.

Q170 On July 20, 1983, Charley Hudson took a no-hitter into the ninth inning against Houston. What Astro ended it with a one-out bloop single?

Q171 Darren Daulton had played all of the 1988 season with the Phils until he broke his hand in August of that year. How did the injury occur?

Q172 Darren Daulton began 1986 as the Phils' starting catcher, but a collision at home plate ended his season prematurely on June 21. Who damaged Daulton's knee?

Q173 True or false—Juan Samuel became the only major leaguer to record double figures in doubles, triples, home runs, and stolen bases in each of his first four big league seasons.

Q174 Why was Kevin Gross suspended for ten days in August 1987?

PHILADELPHIA PHILLIES

A159 Manny Trillo

A160 37 years old

A161 Richie Hebner

A162 Tommy Hutton

A163 Boston Red Sox (1967)

A164 None (In 899 appearances, he never started a game.)

A165 Six

A166 Bobby Molinaro

A167 The Houston Colt 45's

A168 Von Hayes

A169 Pete Rose
Joe Morgan
Tony Perez

A170 Craig Reynolds

A171 Daulton broke his hand when he punched the wall in the team's video room.

A172 Mike Heath

A173 True

A174 He was caught using sandpaper to scuff the ball on the mound.

Q175 Juan Samuel was runner-up for 1984 Rookie of the Year honors as voted by the Baseball Writers of America. Who nabbed the award that year?

Q176 Jerry Koosman was the runner-up for the 1968 Rookie of the Year Award. Who edged him out that season?

Q177 Which Phil ace was a teammate of Roger Clemens and Calvin Schiraldi on the 1983 College World Series championship team?

Q178 On the basis of his major-league-best 40 saves in 1987, Steve Bedrosian snared the Cy Young Award. Who did he narrowly defeat for the honor?

Q179 This Phillie, who swatted 12 homers in 209 at-bats in 1987, knocked a homer that eliminated the Mets from the pennant race in the last week of that season. Identify him.

Q180 Curt Ford, Marvin Freeman, and Oil Can Boyd all attended the same Mississippi college. Name the university.

Q181 For what NFL team did Chris James's brother Craig play?

Q182 Which Phillie hit a high note in his career when he made concert-quality violins for a bow-making company in Chicago?

Q183 Ricky Jordan was called up from the minor leagues in mid-1988 and took over at first base. Whom did he replace at that position?

Q184 In what category did Dickie Thon lead all NL shortstops in 1989?

Q185 Name the Phil who as a 12-year-old lost his left big toe in a motorcycle accident.

Q186 Lenny Dykstra swatted his first inside-the-park homer on July 24, 1990. Against what pitcher did he hit the dinger?

Q187 For the first time in his career, Lenny Dykstra went on the disabled list during the 1991 season. What caused his injuries on May 6?

Q188 In 1988, this Phillie was a second-team Academic All-American with a 3.8 average, the highest for any male Baylor athlete. Who is this gentleman and scholar?

Q189 Name the Phillie who was inducted into the Bowling Green University Hall of Fame in 1988.

PHILADELPHIA PHILLIES

A175   Dwight Gooden

A176   Johnny Bench

A177   Bruce Ruffin

A178   Rick Sutcliffe

A179   Luis Aguayo

A180   Jackson State

A181   New England Patriots

A182   Marvin Freeman

A183   Von Hayes (Hayes went on the disabled list and was moved to the outfield upon his return.)

A184   Home runs (15)

A185   Jason Grimsley

A186   David Cone (of the Mets)

A187   A car accident. (Lenny suffered broken ribs, a busted cheekbone, and a broken collarbone, which put him out for two months and 61 games.)

A188   Pat Combs

A189   Roger McDowell

THE UNIFORMS

Q190   In how many consecutive games did Dale Murphy hit safely immediately after being acquired by Philadelphia during the 1989 season?

Q191   In his second start of the 1991 season, Tommy Greene tossed a no-hitter and earned a permanent spot in the Philadelphia rotation. Against what club did Greene throw the no-no?

Q192   Terry Mulholland fired a no-hitter against his former team on August 15, 1990. Against which team did Mulholland gain sweet revenge?

Q193   Who was the last Phillie to be enshrined in the Hall of Fame?

Q194   In 1991, John Kruk led the club in hitting (.294), home runs (21), and RBIs (92). Who was the last Phillie to lead the team in all three categories?

Q195   Wally Backman was drafted by the Mets and played the first nine years of his career with New York. With what two clubs did he play before coming to Philly in 1991?

FYI

Q1   This Phillie pitcher was drafted (but not signed) by three clubs before he was purchased by the Phillies in 1979. His father played pro basketball with the Pistons. Name him.

Q2   How many AL pennants had the Athletics won before the Phillies took their first NL pennant?

Q3   What is significant about the Phillies' nickname?

Q4   In what year did the Phillies break the century mark for the first time in single-season losses?

Q5   What other teams rounded out the National League in 1883, the year the Phillies came into existence?

Q6   What was the Phils' record in 1883?

Q7   Why did the July 8, 1952 All-Star Game at Connie Mack Stadium end up in baseball's history books?

Q8   What well-known politician was in the crowd when the All-Star Game was last held at the Vet, on July 13, 1976?

PHILADELPHIA PHILLIES

A190 Eight

A191 Expos, at Montreal (May 23, 1991)

A192 San Francisco Giants (6–0)

A193 Ferguson Jenkins (1991)

A194 Greg Luzinski (1977)

A195 Minnesota Twins (1989)
Pittsburgh Pirates (1990)

———————————— · ————————————

A1 Bob Ayrault

A2 Six

A3 It is the oldest name in NL history.

A4 1904 (54–100; this was the inaugural season that the major leagues expanded the regular season from 140 games to 154.)

A5 Buffalo Bisons
Boston Beaneaters
Cleveland Spiders
Providence Grays
NY Gothams
Detroit Wolverines

A6 17–81

A7 It is the only All-Star Game to be shortened because of rain. (The AL was awarded a 5–3 victory after five innings.)

A8 President Gerald Ford

Q9   Who won the All-Star Game held at Veterans Stadium in 1976?

Q10   Name the five Phillies who participated in the 1976 All-Star Game at Veterans Stadium.

Q11   Who was named MVP of the 1976 All-Star Game held in Philadelphia?

Q12   The first Phillie game occurred on May 1, 1883. At what location was the historic contest played between the Phils and Providence Grays?

Q13   The Phils changed their address in 1887 when they moved to the Baker Bowl. What unusual design was featured at the park?

Q14   After 51 years, the Phils bid adieu to the Baker Bowl. Which team did they oppose on their final day at the park, June 30, 1938?

Q15   During a doubleheader on August 8, 1903, the bleachers in the Phillies' home park collapsed, killing 12 and injuring 282. Who was the visiting club?

Q16   After the disaster in 1903 at the Baker Bowl, the Phillies were forced to play the remainder of their games in another local facility. Where was their new home?

Q17   On August 18, 1909, a 50-year-old Giant became the oldest player to steal a base in the major leagues when he took second base against the Phillies. Name the geriatric thief.

Q18   From 1917 to 1948, the Phillies were at .500 only once and finished in the cellar 17 times. By what derisive name were the Phillies known?

Q19   The Phillies were part of broadcast history when their game against the Pirates was played on the radio from Forbes Field on August 5, 1921. Who called the game on Pittsburgh station KDKA?

Q20   Philadelphia played at Cincinnati on May 24, 1935, and lost 2–1. Why is the game famous in the annals of major league baseball?

Q21   In 1944–45, team owner Robert Carpenter held a contest to rename the club. By what name was the team unofficially known during 1944–45?

Q22   What was the nickname of the 1950 Philadelphia Phillies?

Q23   In what year was Shibe Park renamed Connie Mack Stadium?

Q24   Who etched his name in the record books when he recorded the last win at Connie Mack Stadium (1970)?

PHILADELPHIA PHILLIES

A9   National League: 7–1

A10   Greg Luzinski
Dave Cash
Larry Bowa
Bob Boone
Mike Schmidt

A11   Cincinnati's George Foster

A12   Recreation Park, 24th Street and Ridge Avenue (The Phils lost, 4–3.)

A13   Cantilevered stands

A14   New York Giants

A15   Boston Braves

A16   Columbia Park

A17   Arlie Latham

A18   "The Phutile Phils"

A19   Harold Arlin

A20   It was the first ML night game.

A21   "The Blue Jays"

A22   "The Whiz Kids"

A23   1953

A24   Dick Selma

Q25   Who belted the last homer at Connie Mack Stadium?

Q26   The Phillies made two changes in the design of their uniform in 1970. What were the alterations?

Q27   In the question cited above, what other event coincided with the logo and uniform changes?

Q28   In what year did the Phillies play their inaugural game at Veterans Stadium?

Q29   The 1971 Phillies were the first NL club to wear this type of apparel. What innovative fashion statement did they bring to the diamond?

Q30   Name the only Phillie who is on record for hitting the replica Liberty bell in the center-field area of Veterans Stadium.

Q31   A total of 55,352 fans attended opening day at Veterans Stadium, making it the second-largest crowd to attend an opening day at a new facility. What club boasts of the largest inaugural attendance?

Q32   Who did the Phillies defeat in their first game at Veterans Stadium?

Q33   Who garnered the first hit in the history of Veterans Stadium?

Q34   Who swatted the first home run at Veterans Stadium?

Q35   Name the winning and losing pitchers in the first game held at Veterans Stadium.

Q36   Who was the first batter in the history of Veterans Stadium?

Q37   Who was the first batter to strike out at Veterans Stadium?

Q38   The first grand slam was knocked out of Veterans Stadium in the second game ever played at the facility. Who hit it?

Q39   Who were Philadelphia Phil and Phyllis?

Q40   Why was the August 21, 1977 Philadelphia-Houston game at the Vet a noteworthy contest in team history?

Q41   Who is credited with the first inside-the-park home run at Veterans Stadium?

Q42   By what name is David Raymond better known?

PHILADELPHIA PHILLIES

A25   Phillie catcher John Bateman (September 29, 1970)

A26   Numbers were added to the uniforms. A baseball orbiting the *P* was placed on the cap.

A27   The team moved from Connie Mack to Veterans Stadium.

A28   1971

A29   Red shoes

A30   Greg Luzinski

A31   Montreal Expos (Olympic Stadium: 57,592; April 15, 1977)

A32   Montreal Expos (4–1)

A33   Larry Bowa (single)

A34   Don Money (April 10, 1971)

A35   Winning: Jim Bunning
Losing: Bill Stoneman
(Joe Hoerner was credited with the save.)

A36   Boots Day

A37   Bill Stoneman

A38   Roger Freed (April 11, 1971)

A39   A pair of 15-foot figures located between the center-field scoreboards that set off a razzle-dazzle show whenever a Phil hit a homer.

A40   It was the Phillies' first-ever Sunday night game at the Vet. (The Phils won, 7–3.)

A41   Don Hahn (September 5, 1971)

A42   The Phillie Phanatic

Q43 To commemorate the Phils' World Series win, the championship banner was raised over the Vet on opening day of the 1981 season, and this ex-Phil tossed the first ball. Who had that honor?

Q44 Why is Craig Drob a noteworthy name in team history?

Q45 The Phillies finished second in the NL East in 1986 behind the Mets. How many games was the team out of first place?

Q46 What does the Paul Owens Award signify?

Q47 On September 19, 1991, the Phils were scheduled to play the Expos at Olympic Stadium, but the game was shifted to the Vet. Why?

Q48 What is the most common surname in Phillie team history?

Q49 What minor league club in the Phillie chain has been affiliated with the team for the longest period?

SETTING THE STANDARD

Q1 Name the Phillie who established a major league mark for pitchers when he homered in four straight starts (1973).

Q2 Who set a record by playing five different positions in All-Star competition?

Q3 Who was the Phillies' first modern-era (post-1900) NL batting champion?

Q4 What onetime Phillie is the owner of the highest single-season batting average in major league history?

Q5 What Phillie established major league baseball's first "iron man" record for consecutive games played?

Q6 Who was the last Phil to hit for the cycle?

Q7 Who tied a major league record by hitting four consecutive doubles in a game?

Q8 What Phillie troika has bragging rights to being the best-hitting outfield in ML history (in 1894)?

PHILADELPHIA PHILLIES

A43   Jim Bunning

A44   As a 21-year-old architecture student at Temple, Drob designed the team's 100th anniversary logo.

A45   21¹/₂

A46   The award is given to the top player and pitcher in the Phillies' minor league system.

A47   A large portion of concrete had fallen at Olympic Stadium.

A48   Miller (13 players)

A49   Spartanburg (since 1961)

---·---

A1   Ken Brett

A2   Pete Rose

A3   Sherwood Magee (1910: .331)

A4   Hugh Duffy (.438)

A5   Fred Luderus (533 consecutive games)

A6   Johnny Callison (June 27, 1963; at Pittsburgh)

A7   Willie Jones (April 20, 1949: at Boston, as a rookie)

A8   Ed Delahanty (.400)
Billy Hamilton (.399)
Sam Thompson (.404)

Q9 Who was the first player to belt two over-the-fence homers at the Phillies' home park, the Baker Bowl, in one game?

Q10 Not only was this Phillie the first player to homer in his initial major league at-bat, he is the only player to accomplish the feat with a grand slam dinger. Name him.

Q11 Name the Phillie who equaled the major league mark in 1978 with two pinch-hit grand slams.

Q12 Who was the last Phil pitcher to belt a grand slam?

Q13 Who was the first major leaguer to belt two home runs in the first inning of a game?

Q14 Who was the first Phillie to homer from both sides of the plate in one game?

Q15 Who has the distinction of being the first Phil in club history to pinch-hit home runs from each side of the plate in one season?

Q16 Before coming to the Phillies, this catcher had broken Yogi Berra's AL record for home runs by a catcher when he swatted 32 in 1982. Name him.

Q17 This outfielder, acquired from the White Sox in 1959 for Gene Freese, was the first Phillie lefty to crack three homers in one game twice (at Chicago, 1965, and against Milwaukee, 1964). Who wielded the big bat?

Q18 Name the Phils' tandem who each homered in five straight games.

Q19 Who is the first Phillie player to swat pinch home runs from both sides of the plate in one season?

Q20 Who was the first Phillie to win Most Valuable Player honors?

Q21 Which Phillie Whiz Kid was named NL MVP in 1950?

Q22 Who was the first relief pitcher to win the NL MVP Award?

Q23 Who was the youngest professional player to win back-to-back honors as the National League MVP as well as the youngest to win the Sporting News Player of the Year in consecutive seasons?

Q24 Who was the first Phillie hurler to toss a no-no at home in the twentieth century?

PHILADELPHIA PHILLIES

A9   Fred Luderus

A10   Bill Duggleby (April 21, 1898)

A11   Davey Johnson

A12   Steve Carlton (May 16, 1984; at L.A.)

A13   Von Hayes (June 11, 1985; vs. Mets)

A14   Steve Jeltz (1989)

A15   Dave Hollins (1990)

A16   Lance Parrish (The following year, Carlton Fisk broke Parrish's record.)

A17   Johnny Callison

A18   Dick Allen (May 27–28, 30—June 1, 1969)
Mike Schmidt (July 6–10, 1979)

A19   Dave Hollins (1990)

A20   Chuck Klein (1932)

A21   Jim Konstanty

A22   Jim Konstanty (1950)

A23   Dale Murphy (1982 and 1983: while playing for Atlanta)

A24   Terry Mulholland

SETTING THE STANDARD

Q25   Who was the Cy Young Award winner in 1983?

Q26   How many saves did Steve Bedrosian record in 1987, the year he snared the Cy Young Award?

Q27   Who is the only player to have pitched in more games than Kent Tekulve (184 saves)?

Q28   What Phillie duo won 55 games in a season—the most ever by two Philadelphia pitchers?

Q29   In his inaugural season with Philly, Steve Carlton established a post-1900 record when he won 45.8 percent of the club's victories (27 of 59). Who held the record previous to Carlton?

Q30   On June 23, 1971, this Phillie pitcher no-hit Cincinnati and cracked two home runs in the same game. Who performed that major league first?

Q31   Playing pro ball from 1881 through 1894, this third baseman still holds the major league record for total chances per game (4.2) and putouts per game (1.6) for a third baseman. He established the NL career record for errors at third base (553), and hit the first homer in postseason play. Name him.

Q32   What major league fielding record did Fresco Thompson establish with the Phillies in 1929?

Q33   This Phillie was the first regular center fielder to ever field 1.000, and only the third outfielder overall. Name the player who led all National League outfielders in fielding average three times.

Q34   What Philly hurler set a National League fielding record for pitchers by going 274 consecutive errorless games?

Q35   Identify the Phillie who topped all National League catchers in assists in 1963, 1965, and 1967, and established a league standard with 99 consecutive error-free games during the 1966 and 1967 seasons.

Q36   Name the Philly infielder who set a NL record when he successfully accepted 18 chances at second base in one game.

Q37   Who was the Phillie who set a post-1900 major league record by committing 81 errors as a shortstop in 1903?

Q38   Who set a major league record for outfielders with 266 consecutive errorless games?

PHILADELPHIA PHILLIES

A25 John Denny (19–6, 2.45 ERA)

A26 40

A27 Hoyt Wilhelm

A28 Grover Alexander (33)
Eppa Rixey (22)
(1916)

A29 Cy Young (1901: Young had 33 of the Braves' 79 victories, or 41.8 percent of the club's wins.)

A30 Rick Wise

A31 Jerry Denny

A32 He was the first second baseman to have 900-plus chances in three consecutive seasons. (The mark has been equaled twice, but never surpassed.)

A33 Tony Gonzalez

A34 Rawley Eastwick

A35 Clay Dalrymple

A36 Terry Harmon (June 12, 1971)

A37 Rudy Hulswitt

A38 Don Demeter (from September 1962 with Philadelphia through July 1965 with the Tigers)

SETTING THE STANDARD

Q39   Mickey Morandini entered the record books in 1992 when he made an unassisted triple play on September 21 in a game against the Pirates. Name the three Pittsburgh players involved in the play.

Q40   Who is the only second baseman besides Philadelphia's Mickey Morandini to turn a triple play?

Q41   Mickey Morandini's unassisted triple play in 1992 was the first in the majors since July 30, 1968. Name the Washington Senator who turned the play 24 years earlier.

Q42   In 1992, Darren Daulton became the first left-handed Phillie in 26 years to drive in more than 100 runs. Who was the last southpaw before Daulton to break the century mark?

Q43   In what year did the Phils record 200 stolen bases?

Q44   This leadoff man set a Phillie rookie record in 1982 with 42 stolen bases. Name him.

Q45   Who was the Phillie who set a major league record for a 154-game season when he struck out 136 times?

Q46   Bob Dernier is the last Phil to steal home. Against what team did the noteworthy theft occur?

Q47   In the "Year of the Hitter" (1930), National League teams averaged .303 and were led by the Phillies' .315 team batting average. Despite the plate power, the club finished last because of the highest earned-run average by a pitching staff in modern baseball history. What is this all-time mark?

Q48   The Phillies set a record they would like to forget as the team lost a league-high 23 straight games. In what year did the club set that dubious mark?

Q49   The Phillies have the distinction of being the champion cellar-dwellers in the National League. How many last-place finishes does the club have?

Q50   In 1991, the Phils led the majors with 25 extra-inning games. How many resulted in a "W"?

PHILADELPHIA PHILLIES

A39   (1) Jeff King's line drive was caught by Morandini.
(2) Andy Van Slyke was doubled up going from second to third.
(3) Barry Bonds was tagged by Morandini going from first to second.

A40   Indian Bill Wambsganss (Game 5 of the 1920 World Series: Cleveland vs. the Brooklyn Dodgers)

A41   Ron Hansen (at Cleveland)

A42   Bill White (1966: 103)

A43   1908

A44   Bob Dernier

A45   Pancho Herrera

A46   San Francisco (August 29, 1988)

A47   6.70

A48   1961

A49   24

A50   16 (a team record)

Q1 The first president to take in a World Series game saw the Phillies at home. Who was the commander in chief in attendance?

Q2 Four Phillies share the record for total number of doubles (7) hit during Championship Series. Name them.

Q3 Pete Rose is second on the all-time list for career total bases (63) in Championship Series. Who is first, with 75 total bases?

Q4 The Baker Bowl was the site of the first World Series appearance by the home boys. Which team defeated the Phils for the 1915 title in five games?

Q5 In the first game of the 1915 World Series, Babe Ruth made the first of 15 career appearances in the fall classic. What position did the Bambino play that first time?

Q6 What was the total number of runs that the Phillies lost the 1915 World Series by?

Q7 Who did the Phillies edge out by one game on the last day of the season to take the 1950 National League pennant?

Q8 Whose 10th-inning homer against Brooklyn gave the Phillies the 1950 National League pennant?

Q9 Who swept the Phillies in four games to capture the World Series crown in 1950?

Q10 The Phillies' starter in Game 1 of the 1950 Series was a pitcher who did not make one start during the entire regular season. Who was he?

Q11 The second game of the 1950 Series was tied 1–1 after nine innings. Name the Yankee whose 10th-inning homer won it for New York.

Q12 Whose eighth-inning error in Game 3 of the 1950 Series allowed the Yankees to tie the score at 2–2 and eventually cost the Phillies the game?

Q13 Danny Ozark led the 1976 Phils to the NL East Division title with 101 wins, a franchise record. How many victories did World Series winner Cincinnati chalk up that year?

Q14 When the Phillies lost the 1977 NL Championship Series, they achieved a dubious first. What was that?

PHILADELPHIA PHILLIES

A1   Woodrow Wilson (October 9, 1915: vs. Boston)

A2   Richie Hebner
Hal McRae
Pete Rose
Mike Schmidt

A3   George Brett

A4   Boston Red Sox

A5   Pinch hitter (Ruth's only appearance was as a pinch hitter for Brave pitcher Ernie Shore in the ninth inning of Game 1. He grounded out in his only at-bat.)

A6   Four (Game 2: 2–1
              Game 3: 2–1
              Game 4: 2–1
              Game 5: 5–4)

A7   Brooklyn Dodgers

A8   Dick Sisler's

A9   New York Yankees

A10   Jim Konstanty (Konstanty tossed a 4-hitter, but the Phillies lost 1–0. Only six hits were given up in the entire game.)

A11   Joe DiMaggio

A12   Shortstop Granny Hamner

A13   102

A14   The Phillies were the first club to win the initial game of a Championship Series on the opposing team's home field and then go on to lose the series.

Q15   The first game of the 1977 NLCS matched the winner and runner-up for that season's Cy Young Award. Steve Carlton was awarded the honor following the 1977 World Series. Who placed second for the Cy Young?

Q16   Whose first-inning homer in Game 1 of the 1977 NL Championship Series posted Philadelphia to a 2–0 lead?

Q17   The Phillies took a 3–2 lead in the second inning of Game 3 of the 1977 NL Championship Series when a trio of Phillies were walked with the bases loaded. Who was the Dodger pitcher who gave up the free passes?

Q18   After falling behind in the 1978 NLCS (two games to none), the Phils jumped to a 4–1 lead in the second inning of Game 3. Whose 3-run homer propelled Philadelphia to its eventual victory?

Q19   In the first inning of Game 4 in the 1978 NLCS, the Phillies loaded the bases up with none out. Which Dodger pitcher escaped the inning without giving up a run?

Q20   The Phillies tied up Game 4 of the 1978 NLCS in the top of the seventh inning with a solo home run. Who hit the fence-clearer that evened the score at 3–3?

Q21   Of the five games played in the 1980 National League Championship Series, how many went into extra innings?

Q22   The Phillies trailed 1–0 going into the sixth inning of the 1980 NLCS first game. Whose 2-run homer moved Philadelphia ahead of Houston and on to eventual victory?

Q23   In the second game of the 1980 NLCS, the score was tied 3–3 in the ninth inning when a base-running blunder cost the Phillies a chance to win the game. Whose pickoff resulted in an eventual Astro win?

Q24   The third game of the 1980 NLCS ended in the 11th inning with a 1–0 Philadelphia victory. Who had the game-winning RBI and who scored from third base?

Q25   Two Phillies scored in the top of the 10th inning in Game 4 of the 1980 NLCS to give them a 5–3 victory. Name the players who crossed home in the extra inning.

Q26   In the 1980 NLCS, the Phils and Houston were tied 7–7 at the end of nine innings in Game 5. This ace pitched two perfect relief innings and his teammate drove in Del Unser for the team's first pennant since 1950. What two Comeback Kids propelled the team to victory?

PHILADELPHIA PHILLIES

A15 L.A.'s Tommy John

A16 Greg Luzinski's

A17 Burt Hooton (The three consecutive run-scoring walks were given up to Larry Christenson, Bake McBride, and Larry Bowa.)

A18 Steve Carlton's

A19 Doug Rau

A20 Bake McBride (pinch-hitting for Warren Brusstar)

A21 Four

A22 Greg Luzinski's

A23 Bake McBride's

A24 Dennis Walling hit the game-winning sacrifice fly. Rafael Landestoy, pinch-running for Joe Morgan, scored from third base.

A25 Pete Rose
Greg Luzinski

A26 Pitcher: Dick Ruthven
Hitter: Garry Maddox

Q27 This right-hander was the starting pitcher in Games 5 of the 1980 LCS and World Series, and even though both games were won by the Phils, he had no decisions. Identify this ace.

Q28 Until 1980, only two of the 16 teams playing major league baseball in 1903 had still not won the World Series. After the Phillies' victory in 1980, only one was left. What club owns that distinction?

Q29 In the first game of the 1980 World Series, the Phillies staked the Royals to a 4–0 lead going into the bottom of the third inning. Whose 3-run homer in that frame led Philadelphia back to a 5–4 lead?

Q30 In Game 5 of the 1980 World Series, the bases were loaded in the bottom of the ninth and the Phillies were holding on to a 4–3 score against the Royals. Who did Tug McGraw fan to snare the Phillies victory?

Q31 During the 1980 World Series, this Royal became the first man in history to connect for a pair of two-homer games in one Series. Name him.

Q32 Name the Royal who set a Series record by striking out 12 times against the Phillies in the 1980 fall classic.

Q33 What World Series record did Larry Bowa set in 1980?

Q34 The Phils captured their first World Series in the 98-year history of the franchise in Game 6 of the 1980 Series with a 4–1 win over Kansas City. Name the game-winning pitcher, the reliever who ended the game with a K, and the Phil who had a two-run single in the third.

Q35 On what television show did the Phillies and Royals appear after the 1980 World Series?

Q36 The only run scored in Game 1 of the 1983 NLCS was a first-inning home run. Who hit the four-bagger that gave Philly the 1–0 win over L.A.?

Q37 Game 3 of the 1983 NLCS saw the bats of Philadelphia produce seven runs on only nine hits. Who led the 7–2 victory over the Dodgers with three hits and four RBIs?

Q38 In the first inning of Game 4 in the 1983 NLCS, a 3-run homer led the Phillies to a 7–2 win over the Dodgers and the pennant. Who hit the dinger?

Q39 With the score knotted at 1–1 in the first game of the 1983 World Series, this Phillie hit a homer in the eighth to lead Philadelphia to a 2–1 victory. Who had the game-winning dinger?

PHILADELPHIA PHILLIES

A27 Marty Bystrom

A28 St. Louis Browns (Following the 1953 season, the Brown franchise moved to Baltimore and became the Orioles, winners of three Series since the relocation. But the Browns will never be credited with winning the fall classic.)

A29 Bake McBride

A30 Amos Otis

A31 Willie Aikens

A32 Willie Wilson

A33 Bowa set a record by starting seven double plays.

A34 Winning pitcher: Steve Carlton
Reliever: Tug McGraw
Slugger: Mike Schmidt

A35 "Family Feud"

A36 Mike Schmidt

A37 Gary Matthews

A38 Gary Matthews

A39 Garry Maddox

GLORY DAYS

Q40 Who was the goat in Game 3 of the 1983 World Series when his error allowed Baltimore's winning run to score?

Q41 With the Phillies garnering only eight hits in the first two games of the 1983 Series, manager Paul Owens decided to make a one-player change to stir the team up. Who did he bench, and what player started as a replacement?

Q42 Who was the only Phillie to register a victory in the 1983 Series?

TRADES, WAIVES, AND ACQUISITIONS

Q1 How much did Alfred Reach pay to obtain Ed Delahanty from Wheeling of the Tri-State League in 1888?

Q2 In one of the worst trades in Chicago history, the Cubs obtained journeyman Dode Paskert in exchange for this slugger in a 1917 trade. Who came to the City of Brotherly Love in the lopsided swap?

Q3 What baseball legend was acquired by the Phils from the Pirates for Possum Whitted in 1920?

Q4 Where was Dave Bancroft dispatched in 1920 for $100,000, Art Fletcher, and Bill Hubbell?

Q5 What infielder, who later became the Dodgers' general manager, was shipped to the Giants in exchange for Rogers Hornsby in 1927?

Q6 In a trade of first basemen, Don Hurst was shipped to the Cubs in a 1934 deal with Chicago. Who came to the Phils from the Windy City?

Q7 When the Cubs traded this popular player to the Phils for Harry "The Hat" Walker, Chicago fans were outraged. Who came to the Phils in the 1949 swap?

Q8 In 1957 the Phils dealt Del Ennis for Rip Repulski and Bobby Morgan. With what team did they do their wheeling and dealing?

Q9 After the 1959 season, John Buzhardt, Alvin Dark, and Jim Woods were acquired by the Phillies for this slugging outfielder. Who was sent to the Cubs in the transaction?

PHILADELPHIA PHILLIES

A40   Ivan DeJesus

A41   Pete Rose was benched. Tony Perez started Game 3 at first base for Rose. (Perez went 1-for-4 in the Phillies' 3–2 loss.)

A42   John Denny (Game 1: 2–1 win)

A1 $1,900

A2   Cy Williams

A3   Casey Stengel (He played one year in Philly.)

A4   New York Giants

A5   Fresco Thompson

A6   Dolph Camilli

A7   Bill Nicholson

A8   St. Louis Cardinals

A9   Richie Ashburn

TRADES, WAIVES, AND ACQUISITIONS

Q10   When Tony Kubek retired in 1965, the Yanks dealt Phil Linz to the Phillies for this Gold Glove winner. Who left the City of Brotherly Love in the transaction?

Q11   In one of the Phillies' best trades, Tony Taylor came to the team from the Cubs for Don Cardwell and Ed Bouchee. Who else came to Philadelphia in the 1960 deal?

Q12   Viewed as one of the worst trades in team history, the Phillies obtained Ruben Gomez and Valmy Thomas from the Giants in exchange for a pitcher who later had great success. Name the ace the Phils sent packing.

Q13   What present-day broadcaster did the Phils trade in 1967 to the Cardinals in exchange for the services of backstop Gene Oliver?

Q14   It was St. Louis's 1969 trade with the Phillies that eventually led to free agency in baseball. Identify the seven players who were supposed to be exchanged in the deal that changed baseball forever.

Q15   When Curt Flood balked at being traded in 1969, he sat out the season. As compensation, the Phillies received three marginal players. Who came to Philadelphia in the deal?

Q16   Curt Flood eventually resumed his career, though it was not with his former team or with the club that had attempted to acquire him through a trade. Where did the "free spirit" settle down?

Q17   This player, who had the last hit and RBI at Connie Mack, was dealt in 1969 to the Cubs for Johnny Callison and Dick Selma. Who was he?

Q18   Who did the Phillies acquire when they dispatched Ken Brett to the Pirates in 1973?

Q19   Name the Vietnam veteran who was obtained by the Phils for Willie Montanez in a 1975 transaction with San Francisco.

Q20   Name the broadcaster who was acquired with Mike Buskey in a 1975 deal with the White Sox for Alan Bannister, Roy Thomas, and Dick Ruthven.

Q21   The second baseman for the Phils' 1977 and '78 championship clubs, Ted Sizemore, was obtained by the team from L.A. for Quincy Hill and this present-day manager. Name the skipper who went to the Left Coast in the 1976 trade.

Q22   Though pitcher Gene Garber had a fairly successful three-plus seasons with Philadelphia, he was traded to Atlanta on June 15, 1978. Name the Brave who returned to the Phillies.

PHILADELPHIA PHILLIES

A10 Ruben Amaro

A11 Cal Neeman

A12 Jack Sanford

A13 Bob Uecker

A14 Curt Flood, Tim McCarver, Byron Browne, and Joe Hoerner were sent from the Cardinals for Dick Allen, Cookie Rojas, and Jerry Johnson.

A15 Greg Goossen
Jerry Terpko
Gene Martin
(None of the three played in the majors after the trade.)

A16 Washington Senators

A17 Oscar Gamble

A18 Dave Cash

A19 Garry Maddox

A20 Jim Kaat

A21 Johnny Oates

A22 Dick Ruthven

TRADES, WAIVES, AND ACQUISITIONS

Q23   How did the Phils obtain Bud Harrelson?

Q24   How did the Phillies acquire Tim McCarver in 1969?

Q25   Philadelphia signed free agent Ed Farmer after the 1981 season off the White Sox roster. Who did Chicago select as compensation for the pitcher?

Q26   Name the backstop who came to the Phils after the club shipped Lonnie Smith (and a player to be named later) to Cleveland in late 1981.

Q27   Who did the Phillies obtain from the Braves to replace Greg Luzinski in the outfield after the Bull was sold to the White Sox?

Q28   Cub Ivan DeJesus's play fell off considerably in 1981 when the Chicago team traded DeJesus's friend and double-play partner. Ultimately, his poor play and bad attitude resulted in the trade that brought him to Philadelphia and reunited him with his pal. Who was DeJesus's infield cohort?

Q29   Arguably the worst trade in Phillie history involved the acquisition of Ivan DeJesus from Chicago. Name the two players the club gave up to acquire the Puerto Rican shortstop.

Q30   Who was dealt to the Phils when the team traded Bake McBride to the Indians in 1981?

Q31   When the Phils dispatched Mark Davis, Mike Krukow, and Charles Penigar to San Francisco in December 1982, they received Joe Morgan and another player in return. Who came east with Morgan?

Q32   Who did the Phillies acquire in late 1982 in a five-for-one deal?

Q33   Who was the "player to be named later" in the deal that sent Ron Reed to the White Sox in 1983?

Q34   In mid-1989, Juan Samuel was sent to the Mets in exchange for a pair of players. What tandem left the Big Apple in the deal with the Mets?

Q35   Whom did the Phils send across the state in return for Kent Tekulve in a 1985 deal with the Pirates?

Q36   It was a pitcher-perfect trade of two right-handers when this player was dealt to the O's for Ken Dixon in a 1987 transaction with the Mariners. Who came east in the trade?

Q37   What right-hander did the Phillies acquire when they shipped Luis Aguayo to the Big Apple in a July 1988 deal with the Yankees?

PHILADELPHIA PHILLIES

A23   He was signed as a free agent in 1979.

A24   He and Curt Flood were swapped to the Phils for Dick Allen in a seven-player trade with the Cardinals.

A25   Joel Skinner

A26   Bo Diaz

A27   Gary Matthews (for Bob Walk)

A28   Manny Trillo

A29   Larry Bowa
Ryne Sandberg

A30   Sid Monge

A31   Al Holland

A32   Von Hayes (The Phillies sent Manny Trillo, George Vukovich, Jay Baller, Julio Franco, and Jerry Willard to Cleveland in the trade.)

A33   Jerry Koosman

A34   Roger McDowell
Len Dykstra

A35   Al Holland

A36   Mike Morgan

A37   Amalio Carreno

TRADES, WAIVES, AND ACQUISITIONS

Q38 Just prior to the 1989 season, Kevin Gross was traded to the Montreal Expos. What two players came to Philly in the deal?

Q39 Ken Howell pitched for the Dodgers for five years before coming to the Phillies in 1989 and registering a 12–12 season. What team traded Howell to Philadelphia?

Q40 Then thirty-four-year-old Dale Murphy was obtained by the Phils in the summer of 1990 from the Braves. Who did the Phils give up in the deal?

Q41 What two players came to the Phils in late 1991 for Von Hayes in a transaction with the Angels?

PHILADELPHIA PHILLIES

A38   Floyd Youmans
          Jeff Parrett

A39   Baltimore Orioles (Howell made a four-day stop in Baltimore but never
          pitched there before coming to Philly.)

A40   Jeff Parrett

A41   Kyle Abbott
          Ruben Amaro

*** FAST FACTS ***

Greg Luzinski opted for a career on the diamond after he rejected more
than 60 football scholarships.

"The Mad Monk," who was christened Russ Meyer, once became so
enraged after being thrown out of a game, he took off his spikes and
threw them at the ceiling, where they stuck. He lasted with the Phillies
from 1949–52.

The Phils were the first NL Eastern Division team to win over 100 games
two years in a row (1976 and '77: 101 victories each season).

Frank Lucchesi did little to distinguish himself as manager of the Phillies
(1970–72: 166–233). While managing Texas in 1977, he was physically
attacked on the field by Ranger second baseman Lenny Randle after he
benched him. The manager had the player arrested for assault and later
sued him for damages. Soon afterward, Lucchesi was fired.

BOWA BY THE NUMBERS:
Fewest Errors in a Season (150-plus games)—9 (NL record)
Highest Career Fielding Percentage—.980 (ML record)
Games Played at Shortstop—2,222 (NL record)
Years leading NL Shortstop in fielding—6

Philadelphia 76ers

PHILADELPHIA 76ERS

NBA Champion 76ers 1966–67

THE SUITS

Q1   As a reflection of the team's desperate state in the seventies, owner Irv Kosloff took out an ad in *Sports Illustrated*. What was Kosloff seeking?

Q2   Which onetime Sixer coach and GM turned author with books called *Pressure Basketball* and *The Coach's Art?*

Q3   Identify the Sixer bench boss who compiled the most successful two-year coaching record in league history (130–33, regular season; 18–10, playoffs).

Q4   This Hall of Famer's resume includes the following: He was an NBA All-Star 12 times, was a head coach, served as a supervisor of league officials, and is the father of an NBA player. Who is he?

Q5   Which Sixer coach insisted on traveling on chartered airlines so the team could avoid early-bird flights and wake-up calls?

Q6   As of 1993, only one Philadelphia coach has been honored as NBA Coach of the Year. What Sixer skipper holds that distinction?

Q7   Who was the Sixers' coach in their inaugural (1963–64) season?

Q8   What Sixer owner died while attending a game in Boston in 1965?

Q9   The 76ers hired Alex Hannum following the 1965–66 season. What club was he coaching just prior to coming to Philadelphia?

PHILADELPHIA 76ERS

A1   A general manager

A2   Jack Ramsay

A3   Alex Hannum (1966–67 and 1967–68)

A4   Dolph Schayes

A5   Alex Hannum

A6   Dolph Schayes

A7   Dolph Schayes

A8   Ike Richman

A9   San Francisco Warriors

*** FAST FACTS ***

In the 142 confrontations (1959–60—1968–69) between Wilt Chamberlain and Bill Russell, the Stilt averaged 28.7 points and 28.7 rebounds to Russell's 23.7 points and 14.5 boards. Chamberlain's teams, however, lost all four seven-game playoffs against Russell.

Clarence Weatherspoon was the first freshman to top the Metro Conference in rebounding since Keith Lee made the national rankings in that category.

Darryl Dawkins, the Sixers' number one pick in the 1975 draft, was the first player ever drafted directly out of high school.

Q10 A power forward with a 6-point average, Alex Hannum played with seven different teams. His skills were more apparent when he became a head coach. Hannum was the only skipper to interrupt Boston's string of championships (11 in 13 years). What two Hannum-coached clubs won NBA crowns in 1958 and 1967?

Q11 To what ABA team did Alex Hannum jump in 1968, the same season Jack Ramsay was brought on board as Sixer GM?

Q12 In what field of study does Dr. Jack Ramsay hold a Ph.D. from the University of Pennsylvania?

Q13 Who is the only coach Jack Ramsay trails in all-time regular-season victories?

Q14 How many times was Jack Ramsay nominated for the Hall of Fame before he was inducted?

Q15 Jack Ramsay is the winningest coach in St. Joseph's University's history, posting a .765 mark. Who is second, at .699?

Q16 Name the two coaches who in the 1972–73 season led the team to its worst record.

Q17 Kevin Loughery ranks second among his peers for the dubious honor of most technical fouls called against an NBA coach (335 since 1970). Who is the all-time leader in this category?

Q18 Why is Paul Lizzo a noteworthy name in team history?

Q19 Kevin Loughery shares the distinction of having had the most head coaching positions in the league. With what other skipper does Loughery hold that longevity mark, with six jobs apiece?

Q20 At what school did Fitz Eugene Dixon serve as the football, tennis, and squash coach in the 1940s and '50s?

Q21 In what year did Irv Kosloff sell the Sixers to Fitz Eugene Dixon?

Q22 What city statue is Fitz Eugene Dixon credited with saving?

Q23 Identify the team that picked University of Maryland alum Gene Shue as the top overall choice in the 1954 draft.

Q24 A mere six games into his rookie season, Gene Shue was traded early in the 1954 season. To what team was Shue dispatched?

PHILADELPHIA 76ERS

A10   1958: St. Louis Hawks
1967: 76ers

A11   Oakland Oaks

A12   Education

A13   Red Auerbach

A14   Three

A15   Jim Lynam

A16   Roy Rubin (4–47)
Devin Loughery (5–26)

A17   Dick Motta (357)

A18   Lizzo was the first full-time assistant coach in franchise history.

A19   Cotton Fitzsimmons

A20   Episcopal Academy (his alma mater)

A21   1976

A22   The "Love" statue on JFK Plaza.

A23   Philadelphia Warriors

A24   New York Knicks

Q25 With what team did Gene Shue begin his professional coaching career?

Q26 How many games into the 1977–78 season was Gene Shue replaced by Billy Cunningham?

Q27 Gene Shue is one of four head coaches to have ever been named Coach of the Year twice. Who are the other three bench bosses so honored?

Q28 Gene Shue was head coach of two teams between the time he left the coach's helm in Philly and when he became the club's general manager. Name the clubs he coached in the interim.

Q29 What was Billy Cunningham's nickname at the University of North Carolina?

Q30 In what eight categories did Billy Cunningham lead the 1968–69 Sixer team?

Q31 Billy Cunningham appeared in four All-Star Games (1968–69, 1969–70, 1970–71, 1971–72). In how many of those illustrious affairs was he chosen to the first team?

Q32 What award did Billy Cunningham capture in 1972–73?

Q33 Billy Cunningham rejoined the Sixers for the 1974–75 campaign after taking two years off to play for an ABA team. With what club did he star?

Q34 When Billy Cunningham took over as bench boss of the Sixers on November 4, 1977, he was the league's youngest coach. How old was he?

Q35 Who was Billy Cunningham's assistant when he became the Sixers' skipper six games into the 1977–78 season?

Q36 How many times did Billy Cunningham coach in the All-Star Game, and how many victories did he have?

Q37 Harold Katz made a substantial gain when he invested in this weight-loss program. In what enterprise did Katz find his fortune?

Q38 On what championship team did Matt Guokas's father play in 1946–47?

Q39 Native son Matt Guokas played at St. Joseph's Prep, attended another school for one year, and transferred back home to St. Joe's before being drafted in 1966. Where did he play for the year he was out of Philly?

PHILADELPHIA 76ERS

A25   Baltimore Bullets (1966–67)

A26   Six (He'd posted a 2–4 record up to that point.)

A27   Bill Fitch (1975–76: Cleveland; 1979–80: Boston)
Don Nelson (1984–85: Milwaukee; Golden State: 1991–92)
Cotton Fitzsimmons (1978–79: Kansas City; 1988–89: Phoenix)

A28   San Diego Clippers (1978–79—1979–80)
Washington Bullets (1980–81—1985–86)

A29   "Kangaroo Kid"

A30   Scoring (24.8 average)
Rebounds (1,050)
Field goals attempted (1,736)
Field goals made (739)
Free throws attempted (754)
Free throws made (566)
Minutes played (3,345)
Total points (2,034)

A31   Three (1971–72 was the only year he was selected to the second team.)

A32   MVP of the ABA

A33   Carolina Cougars

A34   35 years old

A35   Chuck Daly

A36   Cunningham went 4-for-4, winning in 1978, 1980, 1981, and 1983.

A37   Nutri/System

A38   Philadelphia Warriors

A39   University of Miami

Q40   Matt Guokas certainly had a chance to accumulate frequent-flier miles as he played for six teams in his decade-long career. He was a member of the Sixers, Bulls, Rockets, and three clubs that no longer exist. Name those defunct franchises.

Q41   What was Guokas doing when he was tapped for the Sixers' second-in-command role in 1985?

Q42   Fred Carter earned the moniker "Mad Dog" during a practice in which a teammate noted: "That guy is madder than a dog." Who pinned the nickname on him?

Q43   Prior to arriving in Philadelphia as assistant coach in 1987, Fred Carter was an assistant with three NBA teams—Washington, Chicago, and Atlanta. Name the coach with whom he shared responsibilities in each city.

Q44   Jim Lynam's first position with the team was as an assistant coach on June 17, 1985. Who did he replace in that post?

Q45   Jim Lynam was an assistant coach and a head coach in the NBA prior to joining the 76er organization in 1985. Identify the clubs he piloted.

Q46   Jim Lynam inherited an injury-riddled club from Matt Guokas in the middle of the 1987–88 season. The 76ers finished the season with a 36–46 record. Who had a better win-lose percentage for the year, Guokas or Lyman?

Q47   Despite guiding the 1989–90 Sixers to a better-than-expected mark of 53–29 and the Atlantic Division crown, Jim Lynam was edged out for Coach of the Year honors. Who took the award that year?

Q48   In what two Halls of Fame is Jim Lynam an inductee?

Q49   Apparently, shooting instructor Buzz Braman practices what he preaches. He once made 738 consecutive free throws and attempted 250 shots from college three-point range. Of the 250 tries, how many did Braman sink?

Q50   What is the name of the instructional program created by assistant coach Buzz Braman, which is designed to improve shooting skills?

Q51   Under what coach was Doug Moe a two-time All-American at North Carolina?

Q52   With what former college and pro teammate did Doug Moe break into the coaching ranks with the Carolina Cougars of the ABA?

PHILADELPHIA 76ERS

A40 Cincinnati
Kansas City (twice)
Buffalo

A41 He worked as a Sixer broadcaster for four and a half years.

A42 Ray Scott

A43 Kevin Loughery (Loughery was the head coach with the Bullets, Bulls, and Hawks when Carter assisted him.)

A44 Matt Guokas (Guokas vacated the spot when he was selected as head coach.)

A45 Portland Trail Blazers (1981–82: assistant coach)
San Diego Clippers (1983–84—1984–85: head coach)

A46 Guokas (Matt left the club with a 20–23 record for a .465 win-loss percentage, while Lynam had a 16–23 record, for a .410.)

A47 Cotton Fitzsimmons of Phoenix

A48 Those at both St. Joseph's University and the Philadelphia Big 5

A49 246

A50 "Sure Shot"

A51 Frank McGuire

A52 Larry Brown

THE SUITS

Q53 Thanks to the ABA-NBA merger, Doug Moe entered the NBA coaching ranks. What team was he piloting in 1976?

Q54 What team did Doug Moe shepherd to a franchise-best record and the 1988 Midwest Division title?

Q55 The Sixers fired Doug Moe just 56 games into the 1992–93 season. Less then 24 hours earlier, Philly was trounced 149–93. What team hammered the Sixers in such resounding fashion?

Q56 Doug wasn't the only Moe to face unemployment after the Sixers gave him the gate. Who else was dismissed by the team at the same time?

THE UNIFORMS

Q1 Five players' numbers have been retired by the 76ers. To whom will they always belong?

Q2 This Duke star was the first ACC player to score 2,000 points, pass for 500 assists, and grab 500 rebounds. Who racked up these illustrious stats?

Q3 A trio of 76ers have been named All-Star MVP. Name the players honored.

Q4 Who is the only 76er coach to lose a game while coaching the East in the All-Star Game?

Q5 Wilt Chamberlain established a club record when he registered 21 assists in a game against Detroit on February 2, 1968. Who later equaled his mark?

Q6 Name the five 76ers who are in the Basketball Hall of Fame.

Q7 Cleveland State University feted this Sixer when it made his uniform the first to be retired in school history. Who was so honored?

Q8 What former 76er was the last member of the American Basketball Association to play in the NBA?

Q9 Name the 76er who was the first basketball player in Nebraska University history to have his jersey retired.

PHILADELPHIA 76ERS

A53   San Antonio Spurs

A54   Denver Nuggets

A55   Seattle Supersonics

A56   David Moe, Doug's son and one of his assistants

A1   Hal Greer—Number 15
Billy Cunningham—Number 32
Bobby Jones—Number 24
Julius Erving—Number 6
Wilt Chamberlain—Number 13

A2   Johnny Dawkins

A3   Hal Greer (1968), Julius Erving (1977 and 1983), and Charles Barkley (1991)

A4   Gene Shue (1977)

A5   Maurice Cheeks (October 30, 1982: vs. New Jersey)

A6   Dolph Schayes
Hal Greer
Wilt Chamberlain
Billy Cunningham
Julius Erving

A7   Franklin Edwards (Number 14)

A8   Moses Malone

A9   David Hoppen

THE UNIFORMS

Q10   What 76er twosome played together on the 1972 U.S. Olympic Basketball Team in Munich?

Q11   Which tandem made up the Sixers' "Gruesome Twosome"?

Q12   Who is the only 76er, and one of four NBA players, to have gone from the NCAA champion one year to the NBA championship team the next?

Q13   What Sixer was unaffectionately known as "The Boston Strangler" by Celtic fans?

Q14   Which Sixer is a native of Delmenhorst, Germany, and came to the United States as an exchange student?

Q15   What Sixer played the most minutes in the team's first year (1963–64)?

Q16   Hal Greer tried his hand at coaching for one year, 1980–81. What CBA team did he pilot?

Q17   This Sixer, who was dubbed the last of the two-handed set shooters, retired in 1965, coached a year in high school, and returned to the Sixers when Alex Hannum summoned him in 1966. Name the backcourter.

Q18   Johnny Kerr set an NBA "iron man" record (since surpassed) by playing in 834 consecutive games. Name the three teams he played on while setting the mark.

Q19   Who broke Johnny Kerr's NBA "iron man" record of 834 consecutive games?

Q20   Wilt Chamberlain left the University of Kansas before his class had graduated, which made him ineligible for the NBA draft. Where did "Big Norman" play for a season before he joined the NBA?

Q21   Wilt Chamberlain was the third overall pick in the 1959 draft. What two players were chosen ahead of him?

Q22   Wilt Chamberlain came back to Philadelphia in 1964 when the 76ers made a trade with the San Francisco Warriors. Name the three players who were given up to acquire the center.

Q23   What coach did Wilt Chamberlain play under with both the San Francisco Warriors and the 76ers?

Q24   Who did Wilt Chamberlain replace in the pivot when he came to the 76ers in 1964?

PHILADELPHIA 76ERS

A10   Doug Collins
Bobby Jones

A11   Caldwell Jones
Darryl Dawkins

A12   Henry Bibby (Bibby went from UCLA in 1972 to the Knicks in 1973. The others are Bill Russell, San Francisco and Boston; Magic Johnson, Michigan State and Lakers; and Billy Thompson, Louisville and Lakers.)

A13   Andrew Toney

A14   Chris Welp

A15   Hal Greer (3,157 minutes played)

A16   Philadelphia Kings

A17   Larry Costello (He stayed with the club until 1968.)

A18   Syracuse Nationals (1954–55—1963–64)
Philadelphia 76ers (1964–65)
Baltimore Bullets (1965–66)

A19   Randy Smith (906 games)

A20   Chamberlain played one season with the Harlem Globetrotters.

A21   Kansas State's Bob Boozer (Cincinnati—first pick)
Mississippi State's Bailey Howell (Detroit—second choice)

A22   Connie Dierking
Lee Shaffer
Paul Neumann
(plus $150,000)

A23   Alex Hannum

A24   Johnny Kerr

Q25 Which of these records does Wilt Chamberlain NOT hold?
(1) Most Minutes in One Game (64)
(2) Most Complete Games in a Season (79)
(3) Most Consecutive Complete Games in a Season (47)
(4) Highest Average, Minutes per Game in a Season (48.5)

Q26 Wilt Chamberlain once hit 30 field goals in a game for the 76ers. Who was the opponent?

Q27 Wilt Chamberlain led the NBA in two categories during the 1964–65 season: scoring (34.7 ppg) and field goal percentage (.510). What other 76er led the league in a statistical category that season?

Q28 What was the highest scoring average ever achieved by Wilt Chamberlain as a 76er?

Q29 From the 1957–58 to the 1968–69 season, Wilt Chamberlain and Celtic Bill Russell took turns winning the annual rebounding title in the NBA. Who captured the honor in 1956–57, and who broke the Chamberlain-Russell monopoly in 1969–70?

Q30 Among the many records Wilt Chamberlain holds is most points scored by a Sixer in a game. How many did Big Norman hit the hole for in a 1967 game at Chicago?

Q31 In what unlikely category did Wilt Chamberlain top the NBA in 1967–68?

Q32 When the Sixers snared the 1966–67 NBA crown with victories over Cincinnati, Boston, and San Francisco, it marked the first championship for Wilt Chamberlain since high school. At what high school did the Big Dipper excel?

Q33 How many assists did Chamberlain pass off for when he etched his name in the team record books in a February 2, 1968 game against Detroit?

Q34 Name the trio of players who came east in the 1968 deal that sent Wilt Chamberlain to the Lakers.

Q35 How many times did Wilt snag league MVP honors as a Sixer?

Q36 Only two players have played more minutes in their NBA career than Chamberlain. Who are they?

Q37 In what year of his career did Wilt Chamberlain become the NBA's all-time leading scorer?

PHILADELPHIA 76ERS

A25   (1)—It is shared by Laker Norm Nixon and Warrior Eric Floyd

A26   Chicago (December 16, 1967)

A27   Larry Costello (free throw percentage: .877)

A28   33.5 points per game (1965–66)

A29   1956–57: Rochester Royal Maurice Stokes
1969–70: San Diego Rocket Elvin Hayes

A30   68 (December 16)

A31   Assists (with an average of 8.6)

A32   Overbrook High

A33   21

A34   Archie Clark
Darrall Imhoff
Jerry Chambers

A35   Three (1965–66; 1966–67; 1967–68)

A36   Kareem Abdul-Jabbar (57,546)
Elvin Hayes (50,000)
(Wilt Chamberlain played 47,859 minutes.)

A37   Seventh (1965–66)

THE UNIFORMS

Q38   Wilt Chamberlain never fouled out of a professional basketball game, including playoff and All-Star contests. Within 50, how long was his streak?

Q39   How many times did Wilt Chamberlain lead the NBA in minutes played during the season?

Q40   Chamberlain was continually breaking his own rebound records in his tenure with the Sixers. What was the greatest number of boards the Big Dipper grabbed?

Q41   What milestone salary did Wilt Chamberlain reach in 1965?

Q42   What pair of local rookies did the Sixers have on their 1966–67 roster?

Q43   Two players on the 76ers' 1966–67 championship team returned later in their basketball careers to be head coaches of the club. Who are they?

Q44   This All-Star backcourter served a three-year hitch in the army before he made a name for himself at the University of Minnesota. Name this early-day Sixer standout.

Q45   The 1972–73 76ers set an NBA all-time low with a 9–73 win-loss record. Who was the leading scorer on that team?

Q46   These two players were members of the team with the best record in league history—the 1971–72 Lakers—and the worst—the Sixers of 1972–73. Which two hoopsters experienced the highs and lows offered by the NBA?

Q47   After his sophomore season in the NBA, Doug Collins won the 1974–75 Maurice Stokes Award. What did the honor signify?

Q48   Harvey Catchings was one of a small number of players who had been drafted twice by the same team, 1973 (ninth round) and 1974 (third round). Which club opted for Catchings on both occasions?

Q49   A testament to perseverance, Steve Mix hooked on with the Sixers as a free agent in 1973. How many times was he cut by other teams before he became a Philly mainstay?

Q50   Nicknamed "Popcorn," this hoopster was a third-round pick in 1974 as a hardship case at the University of Arizona, was cut after camp, played in the Eastern League, and eventually made the Sixer squad in mid-season. Who was he?

PHILADELPHIA 76ERS

A38 1,218 games

A39 Eight

A40 43 (against Boston on March 6, 1965)

A41 $100,000 (Shortly after, the Celtics announced they were paying Bill Russell $100,001 in salary.)

A42 Bill Melchionni (Villanova)
Matt Guokas (St. Joe's)

A43 Billy Cunningham
Matt Guokas

A44 Archie Clark

A45 Fred "Mad Dog" Carter (20.0 ppg)

A46 John Q. Trapp
Leroy Ellis

A47 Comeback Player of the Year (Because of injuries, he played in only 25 games in his rookie year.)

A48 Sixers (After the 1973 draft, Catchings decided to play in the ABA.)

A49 Five

A50 Corniel Norman

Q51 What eye-opening feat did Darryl Dawkins perform twice as a Sixer—November 13, 1979 at Kansas City and December 5, 1979 at the Spectrum against San Antonio?

Q52 Identify the team that chose Joe Bryant in the first round of the 1975 draft.

Q53 Lloyd Free, who has had many names, was called the "Prince of Mid-Air" thanks to his soaring abilities. What label was given to his high-arching missiles?

Q54 What was the name of the footware store that Lloyd Free owned in Philadelphia?

Q55 In the last few months of the 1976–77 campaign, this Sixer tandem had an average of 50 points per game together. Name the sharpshooting duo.

Q56 Originally a 1972 fourth-round pick of the Knicks, Henry Bibby was purchased by Philly from another team four years later. From what NBA franchise did the Sixers acquire the UCLA product?

Q57 In what category did Julius Erving lead the nation while a junior in college?
(1) Scoring
(2) Rebounding
(3) Assists
(4) Free Throw Percentage

Q58 At what school did Julius Erving play his collegiate ball?

Q59 Which NBA team selected Dr. J in the 1973 collegiate draft?

Q60 With what player did the good doctor share the 1974–75 ABA MVP award?

Q61 During the 1972–73 season, the Doctor became the Squires' head coach for a single game when the regular coach left the team to scout its next opponent. Who did Erving temporarily replace behind the bench?

Q62 Identify the two professional basketball teams that Julius Erving played with before coming to Philadelphia.

Q63 How many ABA scoring titles did Julius Erving win?

Q64 Thanks to the signing of Erving, the Sixers set a league record in 1976–77. What was that mark?

Q65 The 76ers bought Julius Erving in 1976. What reason did the Doctor's previous owner give for selling the game's best player?

PHILADELPHIA 76ERS

A51   He shattered the backboards on each occasion.

A52   Golden State Warriors

A53   "Rainbow Shots"

A54   Free Throw

A55   George McGinnis
Julius Erving

A56   New Orleans Jazz

A57   (2)

A58   University of Massachusetts

A59   Milwaukee Bucks

A60   George McGinnis of the Indiana Pacers

A61   Al Bianchi (Erving's team defeated the Nets, 123–117.)

A62   Virginia Squires
New York Nets
(both of the American Basketball Association)

A63   Three (1972–73
1973–74
1975–76)

A64   The 1976–77 Sixers were the biggest gate attraction in the NBA (632,994).

A65   Roy Boe, an ABA franchise owner, needed the $3 million to cover the NBA
entry fee.

THE UNIFORMS

Q66 On October 21, 1976, Julius Erving made it official and signed on as a Sixer. In a moment of delirium, a fan sprinted onto the court and handed the superstar something. What did the excited patron present to the newest Sixer?

Q67 Name the Sixer who was a teammate of Julius Erving on the 1976 ABA championship team.

Q68 Name the last team the Doctor played against in a Sixer uniform.

Q69 In combined NBA-ABA statistics, only three players have ever scored more than 30,000 points. Dr. J ranks third on the list. Who are the top two on the all-time list?

Q70 In what 1978 Don Knotts movie did Julius Erving make his silver screen debut?

Q71 How many NBA scoring titles did Julius Erving win?

Q72 The Doctor surpassed the 2,000-point plateau five times during his ABA career. How many times did he reach that figure while playing for the 76ers?

Q73 Current NBA skipper Mike Dunleavy had a short stint with the Sixers when he played in 36 games over two seasons, 1976–77, 1977–78. From what school did the Brooklyn native hail?

Q74 In 1977–78, Mike Dunleavy was a player-coach with an All-American Basketball Alliance team. On what club did he hold the dual role?

Q75 Only one player started in all 82 regular-season games for the Sixers in 1977–78. Who was he?

Q76 In 1978–79, this Sixer was the only rookie in the NBA who started all of his team's games. Who was that star freshman?

Q77 What team originally picked Bobby Jones in the first round of the 1974 draft?

Q78 At the end of the 1982–83 season, the league introduced two new awards: Defensive Player of the Year, which was snagged by Milwaukee's Sidney Moncrief, and an honor that was bestowed on Bobby Jones. What prize did the Sixer star sub receive?

Q79 For three straight seasons, Maurice Cheeks was the leader in the Clean Hands Award category. What does the honor represent?

PHILADELPHIA 76ERS

A66 A doctor's bag

A67 Al Skinner

A68 Milwaukee Bucks (who eliminated the Sixers in the first round of the 1987 playoffs)

A69 Kareem Abdul-Jabbar (38,387)
Wilt Chamberlain (31,419)
(Julius Erving had 30,026 points.)

A70 *The Fish That Saved Pittsburgh*

A71 He never led the NBA in scoring.

A72 Twice (1979–80 and 1980–81)

A73 South Carolina

A74 Carolina Lightning

A75 Henry Bibby (Steve Mix saw action in 82 games, but he wasn't a starter.)

A76 Maurice Cheeks

A77 Houston Rockets

A78 The Sixth Man Award

A79 It means a player has more steals than personal fouls. (1986–89)

THE UNIFORMS

Q80 In a 1978–79 Sixers-Nets game that was replayed because of a protest, three players switched teams in the period between the initial game and the replay contest. Which three players were involved in the trade that resulted in the trio playing for both teams in a league game?

Q81 A 1978 third-round pick by the Knicks, this cager played three years in Italy before he signed as a free agent with Philly in 1982. In his first two seasons, he was dubbed the "Kurt Rambis of the East." Name him.

Q82 At what college did Moses Malone distinguish himself on the basketball court?

Q83 On what two ABA clubs did Moses Malone toil?

Q84 How did the Sixers acquire Moses Malone?

Q85 Two players with the surname of Johnson played for the championship edition of the Sixers of 1982–83. Who made up this version of Johnson and Johnson?

Q86 In a nationally televised game, Sedale Threatt was involved in a fight with a Boston Celtic. With what player did he butt heads in the 1986 face-off?

Q87 "Slammin' Sam" Williams was a member of the 1979–80 Arizona State team that sent all of its starters to the NBA. Name the quartet of players who joined Williams in the big league.

Q88 The top pick of the Washington Bullets in the 1980 draft, this cager played with Atlanta, the Ohio Mixers of the CBA, and was signed to a 10-day deal with the Sixers in 1983. Who is he?

Q89 What honor was bestowed on Auburn's Charles Barkley by a panel of broadcasters and writers who covered the Southeastern Conference in the 1980s?

Q90 What was Barkley's nickname when he came out of Auburn as an undergrad in 1984?

Q91 Charles Barkley was the fifth overall pick in the 1984 draft. Name the four players selected ahead of the Auburn forward.

Q92 Who wore Number 34 for the 76ers before Charles Barkley?

Q93 Charles Barkley set a new 76er record when he scored 1,148 points in his rookie year. Whose previous record for a first-year player did he surpass?

PHILADELPHIA 76ERS

A80   Eric Money was traded to the Sixers while Harvey Catchings and Ralph Simpson were swapped to the Nets. The initial game was played on November 8, 1978; it was replayed on March 23, 1979, and the trade occurred on February 7, 1979.

A81   Marc Iavaroni

A82   Malone never attended college.

A83   Utah
St. Louis

A84   The Sixers dealt Caldwell Jones to Houston for the star center and a 1983 first-round pick.

A85   Clemon Johnson
Reggie Johnson

A86   Danny Ainge

A87   Alton Lister (Milwaukee)
Kurt Nimphius (Dallas)
Byron Scott (Lakers)
Lafayette Lever (Portland)

A88   Wes Matthews

A89   SEC Player of the Decade

A90   "The Round Mound of Rebound"

A91   1—Akeem Olajuwon (Houston)
2—Sam Bowie (Portland)
3—Michael Jordan (Chicago)
4—Sam Perkins (Dallas)

A92   Jim Spanarkel (1979–80 season)

A93   Billy Cunningham's (1965–66: 1,143 points)

Q11. To what ABA team did Alex Hannum jump in 1968?

PHILADELPHIA 76ERS

Q51. What eye-opening feat did Darryl Dawkins perform twice as a Sixer—November 13, 1979 at Kansas City and December 5, 1979 at the Spectrum against San Antonio?

Q49. A testament to perseverance, Steve Mix hooked on with the Sixers as a free agent in 1973. How many times was he cut by other teams before he became a Philly mainstay?

Q59. What NBA team selected Dr. J in the 1973 collegiate draft?

THE UNIFORMS

Q94 Though Barkley had more first-place votes than any other player, he was runner-up for the 1989–90 NBA Most Valuable Player. Who edged him out for the honor?

Q95 In how many consecutive All-Star Games did Charles Barkley play while with the 76ers?

Q96 Charles Barkley earned his All-Star MVP selection when he popped in 17 points, cleared 22 boards, and dished out 4 feeds as he spearheaded the East to a 116–114 triumph. Sir Charles's rebound figure was the most since this superstar grabbed 22 off the glass in the 1967 game. Whose mark did Barkley equal?

Q97 Charles Barkley's life changed on June 17, 1992, for two reasons. It was the day that he was traded to the Phoenix Suns. What other major event took place in his life on that date?

Q98 In a three-for-one deal, Charles Barkley was shipped out to Phoenix. Name the trio who came to Philly in return.

Q99 At the time Charles Barkley left the 76ers in 1992, he ranked second as the NBA's all-time field goal percentage shooter (57.6 percent). Who is first in this category?

Q100 What Sixer cleaned up when he was featured in a commercial for Ivory soap?

Q101 Jeff Ruland forfeited his senior year of eligibility at Iona and played the 1980–81 season in a more exotic locale. Where did he suit up?

Q102 Identify this well-traveled athlete: He was chosen by the Knicks in the fourth round of the 1984 draft out of UC-Irvine, played for Madrid in the Spanish League, re-signed with New York, and eventually hooked up with the Sixers as a free agent in late 1987.

Q103 Name the 76er who was a member of the 1988 U.S. Olympic Basketball Team.

Q104 On what other team did Derek Smith play for Jim Lynam in the mid-eighties?

Q105 Hersey Hawkins led the NCAA in scoring in his senior year of college (1988). For what university did he play?

Q106 What club originally selected Hersey Hawkins as the sixth overall pick in the 1988 draft?

PHILADELPHIA 76ERS

A94   Magic Johnson

A95   Six (1986–87—1991–92)

A96   Wilt Chamberlain's

A97   He was acquitted of battery and disorderly conduct charges by a Milwaukee jury.

A98   Jeff Hornacek
Tim Perry
Andrew Lang

A99   Artis Gilmore (59.9%)

A100 Danny Vranes

A101 Spain

A102 Bob Thornton

A103 Hersey Hawkins

A104 San Diego/Los Angeles Clippers

A105 Bradley University (in Peoria, Ill.)

A106 L.A. Clippers (After he was selected by L.A., Philadelphia sent the Clippers its third pick and a 1989 first-round pick for him on draft day, 1988.)

Q107 The 1988–89 campaign was a memorable one for Mike Gminski as he led the Sixers at the charity stripe with a .871 mark. The G-man also did something that season that none of his teammates could match. What did he accomplish?

Q108 Ron Anderson never played high school basketball. He was spotted playing sandlot ball by a Santa Barbara CC player and convinced to play for the school. What was the 21-year-old's profession before going to college?

Q109 Name the two other NBA teams that 76er forward Ron Anderson played with prior to joining Philadelphia in 1988.

Q110 When Scott Brooks suited up for the Sixers in 1988–89, it was an encore appearance for the free agent out of UC-Irvine. Two years before, the club cut him from its veterans' camp. For what team did Brooks play in the interim?

Q111 Who broke Johnny Dawkins's career scoring record at Duke University?

Q112 When Kenny Payne was selected with the 19th overall pick by Philadelphia in the 1989 draft, he was the second Louisville alumnus to be chosen in the first round that year. Who was the first Cardinal to go in that draft?

Q113 With what USBL team did Manute Bol play prior to entering the NBA in 1985?

Q114 Manute Bol is the tallest player in the history of the NBA (7'7"). Who was the tallest before the Sudanese native arrived on the court?

Q115 Who is the NBA's shortest player?

Q116 What did the 76ers give up to acquire Manute Bol from Golden State?

Q117 In his first NBA season, Manute Bol led the league with 397 shots blocked, the second-highest single-season total in NBA history. Who established the league mark of 456 blocks in one year?

Q118 Manute Bol has registered 15 blocked shots in a game twice—versus Atlanta in 1986 and against Indiana in 1987. Who is the only NBA player to have more blocked shots in a game?

Q119 Manute Bol has three sons—Abuk, Madut, and Chris. Who did he name Chris after?

PHILADELPHIA 76ERS

A107   Gminski started and played in all 82 games.

A108   He was a grocery clerk.

A109   Cleveland Cavaliers (1984–85)
Indiana Pacers (1985–88)

A110   Albany Patroons of the CBA

A111   Christian Laettner

A112   Pervis Ellison (the first overall pick, selected by Sacramento)

A113   Rhode Island Gulls

A114   Utah's Mark Eaton (7'4")

A115   Tyrone "Muggsy" Bogues (5'3")

A116   A 1991 first-round draft pick

A117   Utah's Mark Eaton (1984–85)

A118   Laker Elmore Smith (1973: 17 blocked shots)

A119   Golden State's Chris Mullin (Bol's former teammate)

*** FAST FACTS ***

Jeff Hornacek entered Iowa State as a walk-on in 1981–82 and earned a scholarship the following season.

In Moses Malone's first year with the Sixers (1982), he racked up more points and rebounds than the combined efforts of Darryl Dawkins and Caldwell Jones in the previous campaign.

As a member of the two UCLA NCAA championship teams, Henry Bibby's club lost only three games in 90 starts.

THE UNIFORMS

Q120 On January 24, 1993, Atong Bol stole the spotlight from her husband. What did the 5'7" spouse of the 76er center do?

Q121 Armon Gilliam was the second overall selection in the 1987 draft. What team picked Gilliam and who was chosen ahead of the UNLV forward?

Q122 Charles Shackleford played two seasons with the New Jersey Nets (1988–89 and 1989–90) before he was released and signed as a free agent with Philadelphia in 1991. Where did he play in the interim?

Q123 Nicknamed "Waterbug," this guard was the recipient of the Varsity T Award as Trenton State's best athlete. Who is this New Jersey native?

Q124 This Sixer married his Florida State classmate, a world-class sprinter who ran for the Canadian team at the 1984 summer Olympics. Who is Marita Payne's husband?

Q125 Which Sixer is married to a former Lady Razorback basketball star?

Q126 Clarence Weatherspoon has the distinction of being the second player to have his number retired at the University of Southern Mississippi. What football player was the first to be so honored?

Q127 In the season before he was traded to the Sixers, Jeff Hornacek shone brightly as he led the Suns in five categories: scoring (20.1), steals (1.95), minutes played (38.0), three-point percentage (.429), and what other category?

Q128 In 1993, Julius Erving was enshrined in the Basketball Hall of Fame with seven other roundball superstars. Two of the inductees are women. Who are they?

FYI

Q1 What franchise was purchased in the spring of 1963 and relocated to the CIty of Brotherly Love?

Q2 Why is Walter Stahlberg of West Collingswood, N.J., a significant name in 76er history?

PHILADELPHIA 76ERS

A120   She won $486,000 playing a high-tech slot machine at the Trump Taj Mahal in Atlantic City. (The amount was little more than 25 percent of Manute's annual salary with the 76ers.)

A121   Gilliam was drafted by Phoenix. San Antonio selected David Robinson with the first overall pick.

A122   Italy (with Phonola Caserta)

A123   Greg Grant

A124   Mitchell Wiggins

A125   Andrew Lang

A126   Ray Guy

A127   Free throw percentage (.886)

A128   Ann Meyers
Juliana Semenova (Walt Bellamy, Dan Issel, Dick McGuire, Calvin Murphy, and Bill Walton also entered the hallowed halls in Springfield, Mass.)

———————————   ·   ———————————

A1   Syracuse Nationals

A2   He won a 1963 contest to name the team.

Q3   The year that the 76ers were born was the same year that the NBA experienced a changing of the guard. Who were the outgoing and incoming presidents of the league that season?

Q4   What other franchise changed cities the same year the club moved to Philadelphia?

Q5   What was the top price to see the Sixers in action at Convention Hall in 1963–64, the team's debut season?

Q6   In the Sixers' first-ever game, this Hall of Famer paced the team with 26 points, which helped defeat the Pistons at Cobo Hall. Who led Philly to the franchise's first victory?

Q7   Despite winning their first-ever road game, the Sixers had a rough time away from the friendly confines of Convention Hall. How many victories on the road did the team rack up in their inaugural season?

Q8   Where did the first edition of the Sixers finish in the Eastern Division standings at the completion of the 1963–64 season?

Q9   The 1965–66 76ers took first place in the Eastern Division, edging out the Celtics by one game in the standings. How long was Boston's reign as Eastern Division champ before it was dethroned by Philly?

Q10   In what season did the Sixers move from Convention Hall to the Spectrum?

Q11   What onetime Sixer president is credited with naming the Spectrum and designing the team's scoreboard and foul board?

Q12   How many consecutive games did the Sixers win in their dreadful 1972–73 season of nine wins and 73 losses?

Q13   On November 8, 1978, the Sixers beat the New Jersey Nets in triple overtime. With 5:50 left on the third quarter, a protest was made because the refs erred in assessing technical fouls to two Sixers. Who was slapped with the incorrect calls?

Q14   Because of the team's inconsistency during the 1981–82 season, *Phil. Inquirer* columnist Bill Lyon referred to the Sixers by this derogatory name. What did Lyon label the club?

Q15   Name the Sixer announcer who had his microphone retired by the 76ers.

Q16   Besides the Sixers, five other NBA franchises sport red, white, and blue team colors. Name the clubs that show their patriotic colors.

PHILADELPHIA 76ERS

A3   Maurice Podoloff (at that time the NBA's first and only president) left office that year. J. Walter Kennedy assumed the position.

A4   The Zephyrs left Chicago to become the Baltimore Bullets.

A5 $3.50 (The cheapest seat was $1.50.)

A6   Hal Greer (October 16, 1963)

A7   12

A8   Third (behind Boston and Cincinnati)

A9   Nine years (1956–57—1964–65)

A10   1967–68

A11   Lou Scheinfeld

A12   Two consecutive wins (was their season high).

A13   Coach Kevin Loughery
Bernard King
(The game was replayed and the Sixers prevailed.)

A14   "Team Schizo"

A15   Dave Zinkoff

A16   Detroit
New Jersey
Washington
L.A. Clippers
Sacramento

SETTING THE STANDARD

Q1   Who established a club record by playing in 11 consecutive All-Star Games?

Q2   Name the Sixer who made the city proud by earning MVP honors at the 1968 All-Star Game after he was 8-for-8 from the floor.

Q3   Who won the MVP Award in the 1976 All-Star Game held in Philadelphia?

Q4   Only once in team history have the Sixers not had a representative play on the East All-Star squad. In what year was Philly denied a slot on the team?

Q5   Who was the only Sixer to appear in the 1975 All-Star Game?

Q6   Who was the first player in NBA history to block 300 shots in each of his first two seasons?

Q7   Name the two 76ers who established a Philadelphia record by hitting 21 free throws in a single game.

Q8   Practice must have made perfect for this Sixer when he was 21-for-21 and had a 100 percent free throw percentage. Who set the standard in 1974–75?

Q9   The 1972–73 Philly club had the worst start in the organization's history. How many losses did it open the season with before registering a victory?

Q10   Who leads the Sixer pack in this category: most career personal fouls?

Q11   Who set the club record with 15 disqualifications in a season?

Q12   On December 30, 1977, the 76ers defeated the Bullets at the Spectrum, 126–119. Every Philly player who entered the game recorded double figures in scoring—an NBA first. How many players registered double digits?

Q13   Who is the only 76er besides Wilt Chamberlain to score more than 50 points in one game?

Q14   Name the five players who have totaled more than 10,000 points in a 76er uniform.

Q15   Three Sixer greats are among the top 11 scorers in NBA history. Identify the superstars.

Q16   Who established a club record by scoring 1,196 points in his rookie year?

Q17   Who was the first rookie 76er player to break the 1,000-point barrier?

PHILADELPHIA 76ERS

A1   Julius Erving (1977 through 1987)

A2   Hal Greer (who had a total of 21 points)

A3   Washington's Dave Bing

A4   1974

A5   Steve Mix

A6   Manute Bol (1985–86: 397
                     1986–87: 302)

A7   Moses Malone (February 13, 1985: 21 of 23 vs. New York)
    Charles Barkley (February 9, 1988: 21 of 26 vs. Atlanta)

A8   Don Smith

A9   15 losses (October 10, 1972 to November 10, 1972)

A10   Hal Greer (3,855)

A11   Billy Cunningham (1969–70)

A12   Nine (Doug Collins—23
             George McGinnis—19
             Julius Erving—16
             Henry Bibby—14
             Lloyd Free—12
             Darryl Dawkins—12
             Cadlwell Jones, Steve Mix, and Joe Bryant—10 each.

A13   Moses Malone (November 14, 1984: 51 points vs. Detroit)

A14   Julius Erving (18,364)
    Hal Greer (15,177)
    Charles Barkley (14,184)
    Billy Cunningham (13,626)
    Maurice Cheeks (10,429)

A15   Wilt Chamberlain (No. 2; 31,419 points)
    Moses Malone (No. 8; 23,340 points)
    Hal Greer (No. 11; 21,586 points)

A16   Hersey Hawkins (1988–89)

A17   Luke Jackson (1964–65: 1,126 points)

SETTING THE STANDARD

Q18   Who holds the 76er record for most points in a rookie season?

Q19   What 76er set the team record for most points in a game at the Spectrum?

Q20   As of the 1992–93 season, which opposing player had set the overall record for points in a game played at the Spectrum?

Q21   By four-tenths of a point, this Sixer put his name in the club record books with a 44.8 three-point field goal percentage. Name the sharpshooter.

Q22   Who was the first 76er to register a four-point play (a three-point field goal and a free throw)?

Q23   Who holds the 76er records in single-season three-point baskets attempted (270) and made (108), as well as being the club's all-time leader in three-pointers?

Q24   This player went down in the Sixer record books when he pulled down the most offensive and defensive rebounds in club history. Who was this chairman of the boards?

Q25   Who was the last Sixer to grab 30 rebounds in a game?

Q26   True or false—as of 1992, no Sixer has ever been named NBA Rookie of the Year.

Q27   The team's lowest-scoring loss took place on January 26, 1991, when the Charlotte Hornets' 79 points was enough to defeat the Sixers. How many points did Philly chalk up in the record-setting defeat?

Q28   The highest-scoring game in franchise history occurred at home on January 25, 1970. Against what now-defunct team did the locals roll up a 159–131 regulation-time victory?

Q29   The most points ever scored by the 76ers in a game is 160. Who was the opponent in the contest?

Q30   Since 1963, the 76ers have averaged more than 100 points per game for a season in every year except one. In what year did the club fall below the century mark?

Q31   The largest margin of victory for the 76ers is 54 points. Who did they annihilate in the win?

Q32   The 76ers once lost a game by 48 points, their largest margin of defeat. Who pounded Philly?

PHILADELPHIA 76ERS

A18   Hersey Hawkins (1988–89: 1,196)

A19   Moses Malone (November 14, 1984: 51 pts. vs. Detroit)

A20   Michael Jordan (November 16, 1988: 52 points)

A21   Leon Wood (1985–86; Maurice Cheeks is right behind him at 44.4 percent.)

A22   Henry Bibby (March 2, 1980: vs. Golden State)

A23   Hersey Hawkins

A24   Moses Malone (Offensive: 445 in 1982–83
            Defensive: 749 in 1982–83)

A25   Bill Bridges (32 boards against Seattle on March 19, 1972)

A26   True

A27   75 points

A28   Dan Diego Rockets

A29   SuperSonics (December 20, 1967: at Seattle)

A30   1974–75 (99.8 points a game)

A31   Cleveland Cavaliers (November 2, 1970: 141–87 at Philadelphia)

A32   New York Knicks (November 29, 1972: 139–91 at Philly)

SETTING THE STANDARD

Q33   Name the 76er who is the all-time NBA leader in steals.

Q34   Who set a dubious team record for most turnovers in a season (312)?

GLORY DAYS

Q1   The 76ers won the NBA championship in both the 1966–67 and 1982–83 seasons. Who was each team's leading scorer?

Q2   When Johnny Most repeatedly uttered the famous line "Havlicek stole the ball!" in the deciding game of the 1964–65 playoffs against the Sixers, how many ticks were left on the game clock?

Q3   In the question cited above, to whom did Havlicek deflect the ball after he snatched the inbound pass under the Sixers' basket?

Q4   Identify the Sixer who inbounded the ball and the teammate for whom it was intended.

Q5   After compiling a 55–25 mark in 1965–66, which was enough for a first-place finish over Boston by one game, the Sixers entered postseason play for the first time in team history. Which team burst their bubble with a 4–1 drubbing?

Q6   Which Sixer coach got the ax after the team fell in five games in the 1966 Eastern Conference Finals?

Q7   Name the five starters on the 76ers' 1966–67 championship team.

Q8   The Sixers took the 1966–67 NBA crown after downing the Warriors in six. Which two teams did Philly knock out to make it to the finals?

Q9   With two ticks left on the clock and the NBA title on the line, this Sixer nailed a pair of free throws, giving Philly a 125–122 win over San Francisco at the Cow Palace. Who sank the pressure shots?

Q10   It was no repeat for the Sixers in the 1967–68 finals as the Celtics crushed Philly's one-and-a-half-year "dynasty" by rallying from a 3–1 deficit to take the title. In the seventh game, Wilt Chamberlain refused to shoot for the final 24 minutes. By how many points did the Sixers fall short?

PHILADELPHIA 76ERS

A33   Maurice Cheeks (1,942)

A34   George McGinnis (1977–78)

A1   1966–67: Wilt Chamberlain (24.1 points a game)
1982–83: Moses Malone (24.5)

A2   Five

A3   Sam Jones (The Celtics won, 110–109, then beat the Lakers in five games for the title.)

A4   Hal Greer inbounded the ball; it was meant for Chet Walker.

A5   Boston Celtics

A6   Dolph Schayes

A7   Wilt Chamberlain
Wali Jones
Hal Greer
Chet Walker
Luke Jackson

A8   Cincinnati Royals
Boston Celtics

A9   Chet Walker (in the sixth game of the series)

A10   Four (100–96)

Q11   The Sixers-Celtics title series was postponed by three days because of a tragic event that occurred on April 4, 1968. What happened?

Q12   Home court was no advantage for the Sixers in the seventh game of the 1967–68 semifinals. With the Celtics ahead 98–96 and time running out, two Sixers had an opportunity to hit the hole. Which pair of players missed their golden opportunity, ensuring Boston's win?

Q13   Julius Erving led the Sixers to the finals in the Doctor's first year with the team (1976). In an ironic twist, a former Philly staffer came back to haunt his old team. Which team defeated the Sixers in seven games?

Q14   In the sixth game of the 1978 Eastern Conference Finals, the Bullets were tied with Philly at 99 with 12 seconds left in the game. Whose tip-in gave Washington a 101–99 victory and the series championship?

Q15   Name the Boston roundballer who engaged in a fight with some of Philly's fans in Game 6 of the 1980–81 Eastern finals at the Spectrum.

Q16   What NBA teams did the 76ers defeat in the 1983 playoffs on their way to the NBA championship?

Q17   Billy Cunningham credited Moses Malone with being the difference in the Philadelphia-Lakers championship series of 1982–83. Malone outscored Abdul-Jabbar, 103–94, in the finals. Malone also cleared the glass 72 times in the matchup. How many boards did Kareem record?

Q18   The Sixers won their 1982–83 title in convincing fashion. Of the 13 playoff games in which the Sixers were involved, how many did they win?

Q19   It was no encore—the defending champs fell in the first round in five games as this team won three games in Philadelphia. Which club humbled the Sixers in the 1983–84 playoffs?

Q20   Which team were the Sixers playing when only 6,704 fans attended Game 7 in a 1991 playoff contest?

PHILADELPHIA 76ERS

A11   Martin Luther King, Jr. was assassinated.

A12   Chet Walker (shot blocked by Bill Russell)
Hal Greer (missed shot)

A13   Portland Trail Blazers (who were coached by Jack Ramsay)

A14   Wes Unseld (The Bullet center followed up his own shot to score the winner.)

A15   Cedric Maxwell

A16   New York Knicks
Milwaukee Bucks
L.A. Lakers

A17   30

A18   12 (Philadelphia–Knicks: 4–0
Philadelphia–Bucks: 4–1
Philadelphia–Lakers: 4–0)

A19   New Jersey Nets

A20   Milwaukee Bucks

TRADES, WAIVES, AND ACQUISITIONS

Q1   Who was the first player from Penn State drafted by the Sixers?

Q2   Who was the first player ever drafted by the 76ers?

Q3   Who did the Sixers receive in return when they dealt "iron man" Johnny Kerr to the Bullets in 1965?

Q4   From what defunct team did Jack Ramsay acquire Fred Hetzel in return for Craig Raymond and a draft pick in a 1969 transaction?

Q5   Name the Villanova alum who came back to Philadelphia for Chet Walker and Shaler Halimon in a 1969 swap with Chicago.

Q6   What other player came to the Sixers with Kevin Loughery when the team sent Archie Clark to the Bullets in a 1971 deal with Baltimore?

Q7   In a 1972 "block"-buster deal with Milwaukee, this pivot came to the Sixers in return for Wally Jones. Who was that man in the middle?

Q8   Leroy Ellis and John Q. Trapp were acquired by the Sixers in a 1972 transaction with the Lakers. Name the tandem who went to La La Land in return.

Q9   In 1973, the 76ers had two first-round draft selections. Who did the club select with these prime picks?

Q10   Name the journeyman who was traded by the Sixers to Atlanta in late 1974 for center-forward Clyde Lee.

Q11   George McGinnis was sent packing to the Mile High City in a trade that resulted in two players and a draft choice coming to Philly. Which tandem arrived on the scene in the 1978 deal with Denver?

Q12   What did the Sixers sacrifice in order to acquire Lionel Hollins, Portland's 1975 first-round selection?

Q13   Name the players involved in the summer-of-'86 trade that sent Moses Malone to Washington.

Q14   Known for his defensive prowess, this player (and a draft pick) came to the Sixers from Indiana in exchange for Russ Schoene in a 1983 deal. Identify him.

Q15   Name the Sixers' three first-round choices in the 1984 draft.

Q16   The Sixers were wheeling and dealing with the Bullets when they dispatched Leon Wood to the District. Who came to Philly in return?

PHILADELPHIA 76ERS

A1   Dave Wohl (1971)

A2   Lucious Jackson (1964: Pan American University)

A3   Wally Jones

A4   Cincinnati Royals

A5   Jim Washington

A6   Fred Carter

A7   John Block

A8   Mel Counts
Bill Bridges

A9   Doug Collins (Illinois State: First pick overall)
Raymond Lewis (Los Angeles State)

A10   Tom Van Arsdale

A11   Bobby Jones
Ralph Simpson

A12   A 1981 first-round draft pick

A13   Jeff Ruland and Cliff Robinson were dealt to the Sixers from the Bullets for Malone, Terry Catledge, and two number one picks.

A14   Clemon Johnson

A15   Charles Barkley
Leon Wood
Tom Sewell (traded to Washington)

A16   Kenneth Green

TRADES, WAIVES, AND ACQUISITIONS

Q17   In exchange for Hersey Hawkins and a 1989 first-round choice, the 76ers gave up the player they selected with the third overall pick in the 1988 draft. With what team did Philly deal and what player did they surrender in the transaction?

Q18   Ron Anderson was dealt to the Sixers from Indiana in 1988 for the draft rights to this player. Who is he?

Q19   It wasn't a long trip for the quartet of players exchanged between the Nets and Sixers on January 17, 1988. Mike Gminski and Ben Coleman were swapped to Philly for two players in the even-up deal. Name the combo.

Q20   Maurice Cheeks, David Wingate, and Chris Welp all moved to the Lone Star State when the Sixers dealt for Jay Vincent and this player. Who else came to Philly in the summer-of-'89 trade with San Antonio?

Q21   Philadelphia gave up a passel of draft picks to acquire Rick Mahorn in 1989. With what team did the Sixers do business?

Q22   The 76ers gave up their first-round pick in the 1993 college draft to the Phoenix Suns on October 29, 1990. What hoopster did the club obtain?

Q23   Four days after 1991 began, the 76ers acquired forward Armon Gilliam and center David Hoppen from the Charlotte Hornets. Who did Philly give up in the deal?

PHILADELPHIA 76ERS

A17   L.A. Clippers
           Charles Smith

A18   Everette Stephens

A19   Roy Hinson
           Tim McCormick

A20   Johnny Dawkins

A21   Minnesota Timberwolves

A22   Jayson Williams

A23   Mike Gminski

*** FAST FACTS ***

CHAMBERLAIN VS. RUSSELL—1959 THROUGH 1969

	GAMES	REB.	PTS.	AVG.	W/L RECORD
Chamberlain	142	4072	4077	28.7	60–87
Russell	142	3373	2060	23.7	87–60

(Head-to-head matchup of the players while Wilt was with the Warriors, 76ers, and Lakers.)

Manute Bol is a member of the Dinka tribe, the largest and tallest in Sudan. In the Dinka language, "Manute" means "special blessing."

Philadelphia Flyers

PHILADELPHIA FLYERS

THE PHILADELPHIA FLYERS
NATIONAL HOCKEY LEAGUE
1973-74

Top Row - Frank Lewis (Trainer), Andre Dupont, Ross Lonsberry, Dave Schultz, Michel Belhumeur, Bernie Parent, Bob Taylor, Don Saleski, Tom Bladon, Jim McKenzie (Assistant Trainer). Middle Row - Fred Shero (Coach), Terry Crisp, Simon Nolet, Bob Kelly, Rick MacLeish, Barry Ashbee, Bill Barber, Bill Flett, Mike Nykoluk (Assistant Coach). Front Row - Ed Van Impe, Bill Clement, Keith Allen (Vice President-General Manager), Ed Snider (Chairman of the Board), Bobby Clarke, F. Eugene Dixon, Jr. (Vice Chairman), Joseph C. Scott (President), Gary Dornhoefer, Joe Watson.

THE SUITS

Q1 Fred Shero has the best playoff record among Flyer head coaches (48–35, .578). Who has the worst?

Q2 Who is the first former Flyer to be named head coach?

Q3 Who was the first full-time assistant coach in the history of the NHL?

Q4 What club did Keith Allen run prior to taking the coaching position with the Flyers in 1966?

Q5 On·what Stanley Cup team was Vic Stasiuk a player?

Q6 Vic Stasiuk was a member of the famed "Uke Line" while playing in Boston. What trio was on the line?

Q7 Fred Shero played three seasons in the NHL. On what team did he play?

Q8 It was a trade with the Rangers that allowed Fred Shero to move from Philadelphia to the Big Apple. What did New York give to the Flyers for their coach?

Q9 Bob McCammon coached the AHL Maine Mariners for one season before jumping directly behind the Flyers' bench as their head coach. What record did he establish when he won the 1977–78 Calder Cup?

Q10 Bob McCammon was removed from his first term as Flyer head coach midway through the 1978–79 season. What was the club's record at the time of his replacement?

PHILADELPHIA FLYERS

A1   Vic Stasiuk (0–4)

A2   Paul Holmgren (June 1, 1988)

A3   Mike Nykoluk
(His first season behind the Flyer bench was in 1972–73.)

A4   Seattle Totems (of the Western Hockey League)

A5   Detroit Red Wings (1952, 1954, and 1955)

A6   Vic Stasiuk
Johnny Bucyk
Bronco Horvath

A7   New York Rangers (1947–48—1949–50)

A8   The team's first-round draft choice and cash

A9   It was the fist time an expansion team ever won the championship on an established circuit.

A10   22–17–11

*** FAST FACTS ***

BOBBY CLARKE'S FLYER RECORDS —
* Most Seasons: 15
* Most Assists (Season): 119
* Most Games: 1,144
* Most Assists, Game: 5
* Most Career Assists: 852
* Most Career Points: 1,210

RON HEXTALL'S INCREDIBLE ROOKIE SEASON (1986–87) —
* Led the NHL in wins (52), games played (92), minutes (5,339), and save percentage (.902)
* Winner of Vezina Trophy, Conn Smythe Trophy, and Bob Clarke Trophy
* First-Team All-Star
* NHL All-Rookie Team

Q11 Pat Quinn jumped from the playing ranks to the coaching ranks in 1977 when he became Shero's assistant. With what club was Quinn the captain for the two seasons prior to his joining the Flyers?

Q12 When Pat Quinn was made head coach in 1979, he added two Flyers to his staff. Who are they?

Q13 In 1983, Jay Snider was named the Flyers' president and became the youngest man ever to hold that post on an NHL team. How old was he when he assumed the position?

Q14 Ted Sator, who was named assistant coach of the Flyers in 1983, played professional hockey. What team did he play for?

Q15 Where was Ted Sator coaching prior to joining the Philadelphia club as assistant coach in 1983?

Q16 Mike Keenan registered his 100th win as a head coach in his 152nd game—the second-fastest time in league history. Who hit the century mark quicker than Keenan?

Q17 In his first three seasons behind the Philly bench, Mike Keenan accomplished something that no other NHL coach had done. What plateau did Keenan reach?

Q18 Mike Keenan reached a career milestone late in the 1990–91 season while coaching the Blackhawks: He became the third coach in NHL history to register 300 wins within seven years. Who were the first two men to accomplish this?

Q19 Russ Farrell was the first individual since 1967 to be named general manager of an NHL team directly from junior hockey. Who preceded Farrell's jump to the big leagues?

Q20 With what team did Bill Dineen win the Stanley Cup as a player?

Q21 Name the two major league teams that Bill Dineen coached before coming to the Flyers.

Q22 During which month of the 1991–92 season did Bill Dineen replace Paul Holmgren as the Flyers' head coach?

Q23 What position did Bill Dineen hold with the organization immediately prior to accepting the head coaching post?

Q24 Craig Hartsburg was made assistant coach of the Flyers in 1990. With what club did he hold a similar post prior to joining Philadelphia?

PHILADELPHIA FLYERS

A11   Atlanta Flames

A12   Bobby Clarke (assistant coach)
Joe Watson (scout)

A13   26 years old

A14   New York Raiders (of the WHA)

A15   Sweden

A16   Boston's Tom Johnson (1971–72 and 1972–73: 100 victories in 138 contests)

A17   He became the first skipper in league history to win 40 or more games in each of his first three seasons. (1984–85: 53; 1985–86: 53; 1986–87: 46)

A18   Fred Shero
Glen Sather

A19   Wren Blair

A20   Detroit Red Wings (1953–54 and 1954–55)

A21   Houston
New England
(both of the World Hockey Association; he was also head coach of Adirondack in the American Hockey League.)

A22   December (December 4, 1991)

A23   Scout

A24   Minnesota North Stars

THE UNIFORMS

Q1   Name the Flyer who was named Sweden's Athlete of the Year in 1984.

Q2   Who was the first captain in Flyer history?

Q3   Who was the first player to sign a contract with the Flyers?

Q4   Who was the first player to have his jersey retired by the Flyers?

Q5   Who was the first Flyer to marry a woman from the Philadelphia area?

Q6   Who was the first member of the Flyers to ever be inducted into the Hockey Hall of Fame?

Q7   Who was the only flyer to register a hat trick during the 1967–68 season?

Q8   Name the two Flyers who scored within 14 seconds of each other in a January 15, 1968 game against Oakland.

Q9   In the Flyers' inaugural season, this player set the club mark in penalty minutes in one game (34) and penalties in one game (6) during a January 25, 1968 contest against Minnesota. Who is this original "Broad Street Bully"?

Q10   Who were the only two players to play in every Flyer game during the 1967–68 season?

Q11   Two Flyers reached the 20-goal plateau during the 1967–68 season. Who were they?

Q12   What player shared the Bruins' blue-line duties with Hall of Famer Bobby Orr?

Q13   Who led the Flyers in penalty minutes in their first season?

Q14   What club did Bernie Parent play for before arriving in Philadelphia in 1967?

Q15   On January 31, 1971, Bernie Parent was traded to Toronto. What two players came to the Flyers for the netminder (and a second-round pick in the 1971 Amateur Draft)?

Q16   In an encore appearance, the Flyers acquired the rights to Bernie Parent and a draft choice in a 1973 deal with the Leafs. Who went north of the border in return?

Q17   What WHA team selected Bernie Parent in that league's February 1971 player selection draft?

PHILADELPHIA FLYERS

A1   Per-Erik Eklund

A2   Lou Angotti (1967–68)

A3   Bernie Parent

A4   Barry Ashbee (April 3, 1975: November 4)

A5   Andre Lacroix
(In 1969, Lacroix married Sue Postus.)

A6   Bernie Parent (September 25, 1984)

A7   Leon Rochefort (twice)

A8   Brit Selby (7:10 of the third period)
Jean Gauthier (7:24 of the third period)

A9   Forbes Kennedy

A10   John Miszak
Leon Rochefort

A11   Leon Rochefort (21)
Bill Sutherland (20)

A12   Joe Watson (Orr was best man at his defensive partner's wedding.)

A13   Ed Van Impe (141 minutes)

A14   Boston Bruins

A15   Bruce Gamble
Mike Walton
(plus a 1971 first-round draft pick in the Amateur Draft)

A16   Doug Favell (and a first-round draft choice)

A17   Miami Screaming Eagles

THE UNIFORMS

Q18   Name the World Hockey Association club that Bernie Parent played with during the 1972–73 season.

Q19   Bernie Parent played in 73 regular-season games during the 1973–74 season. Who "shared" the Flyer netminding responsibilities that year?

Q20   Bernie Parent set the NHL mark for goaltenders when he played in 73 games during the 1973–74 season. What goaltender has since surpassed his record?

Q21   With whom did Bernie Parent share the 1973–74 Vezina Trophy as the NHL's top goaltender?

Q22   Bernie Parent won back-to-back Vezina Trophies in 1974 and 1975. Who was the last NHL goalie to win the award honoring the league's best netminder in consecutive seasons?

Q23   Who was the next netminder to win consecutive Vezina Trophies after Bernie Parent captured the award in 1974 and 1975?

Q24   On February 17, 1979, Bernie Parent's career came to an end when a stick inadvertently struck the goaltender in the eye. What player ended the Hall of Famer's career?

Q25   Doug Favell missed most of the 1969–70 season due to a freak accident. What caused him to miss all but 15 games that season?

Q26   Ed Van Impe scored only two goals during the 1973–74 season, but both tallies were against the same team. Who fell victim to Ed's "scoring prowess"?

Q27   While playing for Chicago in his rookie season, Ed Van Impe finished second in the 1966–67 NHL Rookie of the Year balloting. Who topped the defenseman for the honor?

Q28   Prior to arriving in Philadelphia, Joe Watson was teamed at the blue line with a future Hall of Famer. Who was Watson's defensive partner?

Q29   Why does Leon Rochefort's name appear in the Flyers' record books?

Q30   Bobby Clarke was the second player selected by the Flyers in the 1969 Amateur Draft. Who did the club choose with its first-round pick that year?

Q31   When Bobby Clarke netted 27 goals in 1970–71, it was the most single-season goals to date of any Flyer. Whose team record did he surpass?

PHILADELPHIA FLYERS

A18   Philadelphia Blazers

A19   Bobby Taylor (He played in part or all of seven games.)

A20   Edmonton's Grant Fuhr (1987–88: 75 games)

A21   Chicago's Tony Esposito

A22   Montreal's Jacques Plante (He won the award five consecutive seasons from 1956 through 1960.)

A23   Montreal's Ken Dryden (1976 through 1979)

A24   Don Maloney (New York Rangers)

A25   He stepped barefoot on a skate blade and severed his Achilles tendon.

A26   Los Angeles Kings

A27   Boston's Bobby Orr

A28   Bobby Orr

A29   He bagged the Flyers' first-ever hat trick (November 4, 1967; vs. Montreal)

A30   Bob Currier

A31   Gary Dornhoffer (1969–70: 26 goals)

*** FAST FACTS ***

Ilkka Sinisalo was the third player in NHL history to score his first career goal on a penalty shot (October 11, 1981: vs. Pittsburgh). The first was Ralph Bowman of the St. Louis Eagles in 1934–35. (Bowman's goal was also the first successful penalty shot in NHL history.) Phil Hoene of the Kings netted his inaugural goal on a penalty shot in 1973.

THE UNIFORMS

Q32   Bobby Clarke was the first Flyer to crack the NHL's top 10 in single-season scoring when he registered 81 points during the 1971–72 year. With what player was Clarke tied for 10th in scoring that year?

Q33   Bobby Clarke was the first Flyer to win an individual NHL award. What trophy did Clarke start his collection with on June 7, 1972?

Q34   In the 1973–74 season, Bobby Clarke was the fifth-highest scorer in the NHL, with 87 points (35 goals, 52 assists). What club boasted of having the top four scorers in the league?

Q35   Bobby Clarke had two separate terms as the team captain—1972–73 to 1978–79, and January 6, 1983 to the end of the 1983–84 season. Who were the two players who held the position between Clarke's tenures?

Q36   Bobby Clarke played in his 1,000th NHL game on October 23, 1982. Who were the Flyers playing that evening?

Q37   Bobby Clark became the 13th player in NHL history to reach the 1,000-point plateau when he scored a third-period goal on March 19, 1981. Who were the Flyers playing that evening?

Q38   In Bobby Clarke's final season (1983–84), he notched his 1,200th NHL point. Against what team did he reach that plateau?

Q39   Bobby Clarke retired at the end of the 1983–84 season as the leading scorer in Flyer history (358 goals, 852 assists: 1210 points). Did Clarke average more or less than one point per game during his career?

Q40   Bobby Clarke was selected by a blue-ribbon panel of hockey executives and past players to *Hockey Magazine*'s Team of the Seventies. Name the six other players who made up the roster.

Q41   Though almost perfect on the ice, Bobby Clarke suffers from an incurable illness. What is his malady?

Q42   Dave Schultz was the first member of the Flyers to ever release a record. What was the name of his 1975 song?

Q43   In what round was Dave Schultz selected by Philadelphia in the 1969 Amateur Draft?

Q44   Barry Ashbee's career came to an end when a shot in the overtime of the fourth Stanley Cup semifinal game struck him in the right eye. What Ranger's shot struck the Flyer defenseman?

PHILADELPHIA FLYERS

A32   Montreal's Jacques Lemaire

A33   Bill Masterton Memorial Trophy
(awarded for perseverance, sportsmanship, and dedication to hockey)

A34   Boston Bruins (Phil Esposito: 145 points
                   Bobby Orr: 122
                   Ken Hodge: 105
                   Wayne Cashman: 89)

A35   Mel Bridgeman (1979–80 and 1980–81)
Bill Barber (1981–82 to January 6, 1983)

A36   The Penguins, at Pittsburgh (Philadelphia lost 4–2.)

A37   Boston Bruins (The Flyers won 5–3 at the Spectrum.)

A38   Boston Bruins (March 15, 1984)

A39   More (Clarke averaged 1.058 points per game in his 1,144-game career.)

A40   Phil Esposito
Guy Lafleur
Bobby Hull
Bobby Orr
Larry Robinson
Ken Dryden

A41   Diabetes

A42   "Penalty Box"

A43   Fifth

A44   Dale Rolfe's

*** FAST FACTS ***

On March 1, 1968, the Flyers were gone with the wind when the roof of the Spectrum blew off and the team was forced to play the final month of the season on the road.

GM Russ Farwell was only the third person to move directly from junior hockey to NHL general manager. Wren Blair (Oshawa to Minnesota in 1967–68) and Leighton "Hap" Emms (Barrie to Boston in 1965–66) were the only others to do so.

Q45 In 1970, Bob Kelly became the second Flyer to jump directly from the amateur ranks to the NHL. Who was the first?

Q46 Rick MacLeish came to Philly in a January 1971 trade with Boston that sent Mike Walton to Beantown. Who accompanied MacLeish to the Flyers in the deal?

Q47 With what club did Rick MacLeish play in his first NHL game?

Q48 On February 5, 1976, Rick MacLeish's season was cut short when he was checked by a Vancouver Canuck and suffered an injured knee in the Spectrum. Who caused him to miss the balance of the season?

Q49 In the first period of a February 1972 game against Vancouver, this Flyer netminder suffered a heart attack. He kept playing and racked up a 3–1 win. Who was this cardiac kid?

Q50 Fred Shero's interest in Andre Dupont began prior to his arrival in Philadelphia in 1972. Where did Shero coach "Moose" before they were reunited in Philly?

Q51 Though he led all rookies in goals (30) and points (34), Bill Barber was second in the 1972–73 Rookie of the Year balloting. Who edged him out for the honor?

Q52 Against what club did Bill Barber score his 300th career goal?

Q53 Against what club did Bill Barber sustain a broken jaw on January 15, 1983?

Q54 What five players were given up to Quebec in the trade that brought Eric Lindros to Philly?

Q55 Terry Crisp hails from Parry Sound, Ont. What other NHL star was born in that city?

Q56 Terry Crisp became the Flyers' assistant coach in the 1977–78 season. Though he played in two games with the club during the previous season, Crisp held another job that year. What was it?

Q57 Who was the leading regular-season goal scorer among the Flyer defensemen on the 1973–74 Stanley Cup-winning club?

Q58 Only five days after winning their first Stanley Cup, the Flyers took a major step to improve the team by acquiring Reggie Leach. What three players were given up to gain the high-scoring forward?

PHILADELPHIA FLYERS

A45   Bobby Clarke

A46   Danny Schock

A47   Philadelphia (He had spent his career in the minors before coming to the Flyers.)

A48   Harold Snepts

A49   Bruce Gamble

A50   Omaha

A51   Ranger Steve Vickers

A52   Detroit Red Wings (November 15, 1980)

A53   Chicago Black Hawks

A54   Ron Hextall
Mike Ricci
Peter Forsberg
Steve Duchesne
Kerry Huffman

A55   Bobby Orr

A56   He was a radio and television commentator.

A57   Tom Bladen (12 goals)

A58   Al MacAdam
George Pesut
Larry Wright
(plus the Flyers' first-round pick in the 1974 draft)

Q59 What club originally drafted Reggie Leach with the third overall pick in the 1970 Amateur Draft?

Q60 By 1974, the Flyers possessed both the third and fourth overall picks in the 1970 Amateur Draft, in Reggie Leach and Rick MacLeish. What two players were selected ahead of them that year?

Q61 When Reggie Leach scored 61 goals in 1975–76, only one other player had netted more goals in a season. Who was that?

Q62 Reggie Leach set an NHL record for right wingers when he netted 61 goals during the 1975–76 season. Who was the first right winger to break Leach's mark?

Q63 Paul Holmgren was the sixth American to reach the NHL's 100 goal plateau when he scored against Hartford on March 29, 1981. Name the five Yankee skaters who preceded Holmgren.

Q64 Paul Holmgren played 500 of his 527 career NHL games in a Flyer uniform. With what team did he play the balance?

Q65 On January 11, 1976, the Flyers became the first NHL club to defeat the visiting Soviet Army team. Among the goals scored by Philly in the 4–1 victory was a shorthanded tally. Who scored that goal?

Q66 Who selected Barry Dean with the second overall selection in the 1975 Amateur Draft?

Q67 Barry Dean played one season in the World Hockey Association. With whom was he playing in the 1975–76 season?

Q68 Ken Linseman played one year (1977–78) in the WHA. With what team did he begin his pro career?

Q69 In what sport did Pete Peeters excel before he devoted himself to hockey full-time?

Q70 Name the pair of Flyers who led the team in assists in the 1979–1980 season, with 57.

Q71 Though Brian Propp was the top freshman scorer during the 1979–80 season (34 goals, 41 assists: 75 points), he did not win the Calder Trophy as the NHL's Rookie of the Year. Who captured the award that season?

Q72 Brian Propp set the major junior hockey career record for points with a three-year total of 511 while playing for Brandon. Who broke his record during the 1986–87 season?

PHILADELPHIA FLYERS

A59 Boston Bruins

A60 Gil Perreault (Buffalo Sabres)
Dale Tallon (Vancouver Canucks)

A61 Phil Esposito (1970–71: 76
1973–74: 68
1971–72: 66)

A62 Islander Mike Bossy (1978–79: 69 goals)

A63 Cecil Dillion
Billy Bruch
Tommy Williams
Charlie Burns
Steve Jensen

A64 Minnesota North Stars

A65 Joe Watson

A66 Kansas City Scouts

A67 Phoenix Roadrunners

A68 Birmingham Bulls

A69 Swimming

A70 Bobby Clarke
Ken Linseman

A71 Boston's Ray Bourque

A72 Rob Brown

Q21. With whom did Bernie Parent share the 1973–74 Vezina Trophy as the NHL's top goaltender?

PHILADELPHIA FLYERS

Q39. Bobby Clarke (shown with Montreal's Guy LaPointe) retired at the end of the 1983–84 season as the leading scorer in Flyer history. Did Clarke average more or less than one point per game during his career?

Q52. Who was the first Flyer defenseman to attempt a penalty shot?

PHILADELPHIA FLYERS

Q4. Who was the first non-goalie selected by the Flyers in the 1967 expansion draft?

Q73 Mike Busniuk was signed as a free agent by the Flyers in 1977 and broke into the club's lineup two years later. What team originally drafted the defenseman in 1971?

Q74 What team drafted Phil Myre with the fifth overall choice in the 1966 Amateur Draft?

Q75 Name the dynamic trio who made up the "Rat Patrol" line.

Q76 In what round was Ron Flockhart drafted by the Flyers?

Q77 Thomas Eriksson opened the 1981–82 season with the Flyers. How many games did he play with Philadelphia before he left to return to Sweden?

Q78 Due to injuries, Tim Kerr played in only eight games during the 1987–88 season. His three goals that season were all scored in one game. Against what club did he register the hat-trick?

Q79 "Flocky Hockey" came to Philadelphia in the early 1980s. Name the players who were on the "Hi-Speed Line."

Q80 What team originally drafted Brad Marsh with the 11th overall choice in the 1978 Amateur Draft?

Q81 As a Maple Leaf, Darryl Sittler made NHL history when he notched 10 points (6 goals, 4 assists) in one game. Who was Toronto's opponent that game?

Q82 Darryl Sittler was acquired by the Flyers on January 20, 1982, for Rick Castello, a second-round in 1982, and a player to be named later. Name the three players Toronto eventually received in the deal.

Q83 Darryl Sittler netted his 400th career goal two months after he joined the Flyers. What club was Philadelphia playing when Darryl reached that plateau?

Q84 Darryl Sittler was shipped off to his third and last NHL club on October 10, 1984. Who did the Flyers obtain in the deal that sent the future Hall of Famer to Detroit?

Q85 What was unique about the first NHL goal scored by Ilkka Sinisalo?

Q86 Pelle Lindbergh tended the Flyer goal in a 0–0 game with the Penguins on December 4, 1982. Who was in the nets for Pittsburgh?

Q87 What club was Philadelphia playing in January 1983 when Pelle Lindbergh sustained a fractured wrist?

PHILADELPHIA FLYERS

A73   Montreal Canadiens

A74   Montreal Canadiens

A75   Ken Linseman
Brian Propp
Paul Holmgren

A76   Flockhart was never drafted. He signed as a free agent with the club.

A77   One (He played in the opening-night game and then announced that he was returning to his homeland because he couldn't adjust to American life.)

A78   Winnipeg Jets

A79   Ron Flockhart
Ray Allison
Brian Propp

A80   Atlanta Flames

A81   Boston Bruins (February 7, 1976)

A82   1982 pick: Peter Ihnacak
Player to be named: Ken Strong

A83   Chicago Black Hawks (March 18, 1982)

A84   Murray Craven
Joe Paterson

A85   It was scored on a penalty shot.

A86   Denis Heron

A87   Soviet Nationals (It was a mid-season exhibition game.)

Q88 In his rookie season (1982–83), Bob Frose put together a string of 13 games without a defeat (12–0–1). What club ended his streak?

Q89 What college did Dave Poulin attend?

Q90 What was unique about the first NHL goal ever scored by Miroslav Dvorak?

Q91 How old was Mark Howe when he played on the Silver Medal-winning U.S. Olympic Team in 1972?

Q92 With what WHA club was Marke Howe teamed up with father Gordie and brother Marty?

Q93 Mark Howe's career was almost cut short due to an injury suffered during the 1980–81 season. What happened to the defenseman?

Q94 Mark Howe was the runner-up for the Norris Trophy in the 1982–83 voting for the league's best defenseman. Who won the honor that year?

Q95 On February 12, 1986, Marke Howe became the Flyers' all-time leading scorer among defensemen when he registered his 231st point. Against what team did he achieve this mark?

Q96 In the 1985–86 season, Mark Howe was the recipient of the Emery Edge Trophy, which honors the NHL's leader in the plus/minus rating. Who was the only player to ever have a better rating than Howe's +85?

Q97 In his first NHL game on December 9, 1982, Ron Sutter scored the game-winning goal. Who was the Flyers' opponent that evening?

Q98 Ron was one of six Sutter brothers to play in the NHL. Name the other five siblings.

Q99 This 1983–84 Flyer defenseman-winger led the NHL in penalty minutes the season prior to arriving in Philadelphia. Name him.

Q100 Dave Brown received a 15-game suspension during the 1987–88 season as a result of a match penalty for high-sticking. Who was on the receiving end of Brown's slash in the incident?

Q101 What team originally drafted Ed Hospodar in the second round of the 1979 NHL Entry Draft?

Q102 What other professional sport did Peter Zezel play besides hockey?

Q103 In what 1986 movie did Peter Zezel appear?

PHILADELPHIA FLYERS

A88   Buffalo Sabres (February 23, 1983)

A89   Notre Dame

A90   It was a short-handed tally. (February 10, 1983: vs. St. Louis)

A91   16 years old

A92   Houston Aeros

A93   He was impaled on the center point of a fallen goal net.

A94   Washington's Rod Langway

A95   Sabres (at Buffalo)

A96   Wayne Gretzky (1984–85: +98)

A97   Quebec Nordiques

A98   Rich (Ron's twin brother)
Darryl
Duane
Brent
Brian

A99   Randy Holt

A100   Ranger Tomas Sandstrom (October 27, 1987)

A101   New York Rangers

A102   Soccer (He played for the Toronto Blizzard of the North American Soccer League.)

A103   *Youngblood*

Q104   In 1987–88, Rick Tocchet became the third player in NHL history to record 30 goals and 300 penalty minutes in the same season. Who were the first two to accomplish this?

Q105   In his first NHL game, on January 8, 1985, Todd Bergen tallied two goals in the Spectrum, including the game-winner. Against what club did he make his debut?

Q106   Chico Resch was acquired from the New Jersey Devils on March 11, 1986. What did Philly have to give up for the 12-year veteran?

Q107   Ron Hextall had three family members who preceded him as NHL players. Name his pro relatives.

Q108   In what round was Ron Hextall drafted by the Flyers in the 1982 Entry Draft?

Q109   Ron Hextall led the NHL in most goaltender categories and was selected as the league's best goalie and the playoff MVP, but could only place in the Rookie of the Year balloting. Who beat Hextall out for the 1987 Calder Memorial Trophy?

Q110   Ron Hextall set an NHL record when he played 1,540 minutes in the 1987 playoffs. Who held the record prior to the Flyer goalie?

Q111   On December 8, 1987, Ron Hextall became the first goalie in NHL history to score a goal. What team was Philly playing at the Spectrum that evening?

Q112   Who tended the Flyers' nets in the 1987 season opener at the Spectrum against Montreal?

Q113   Name the three NHL teams that Willie Huber played for during the 1987–88 season.

Q114   Doug Sulliman was acquired by the Flyers on October 3, 1988, in the NHL waiver draft. Name the three teams he played with before he arrived in Philadelphia.

Q115   What is the name of Eric Lindros's sports biography?

Q116   What precautions did the Flyers take when the club and Eric Lindros faced the Nordiques in Quebec on October 13, 1992?

PHILADELPHIA FLYERS

A104   Vancouver's Tiger Williams (1980–81)
Chicago's Al Secord (1981–82)

A105   Vancouver Canucks

A106   A third-round draft pick in the 1986 Entry Draft

A107   Brayan Hextall, Sr. (grandfather: 1936–37—1947–48)
Bryan Hextall, Jr. (father: 162–63—1975–76)
Dennis Hextall (uncle: 1968–69—1979–80)

A108   Sixth (119th selection overall)

A109   L.A.'s Luc Robitaille

A110   Calgary's Mike Vernon (1986: 1,229 minutes)

A111   Boston Bruins

A112   Mark LaForest (The game ended in a 2–2 tie.)

A113   New York Rangers (11 games)
Vancouver Canucks (35 games)
Flyers (10 games)

A114   N.Y. Rangers (1979–80—1980–81)
Hartford Whalers (1981–82—1983–84)
New Jersey Devils (1984–85—1987–88)

A115   *Fire on Ice*

A116   Philadelphia hired a security guard to escort Lindros.

Q1   Match the opponent with Flyer victory.
       (A) 100th (10/9/71)   (1) Boston Bruins
       (B) 200th (3/12/74)   (2) N.Y. Islanders
       (C) 500th (11/2/80)   (3) Vancouver Canucks
       (D) 800th (1/15/87)   (4) Montreal Canadiens

Q2   Philadelphia and the other five new franchises doubled the size of the NHL in 1967. What were the original six clubs that preceded the expansion?

Q3   Name the other new clubs in 1967.

Q4   What opposing player is credited with scoring the first hat trick against the Flyers?

Q5   The Flyers went six seasons before any player was given a penalty shot against them, and the first one resulted in a goal. Name the opponent who is credited with the initial penalty goal.

Q6   What two clubs defeated the 1975–76 Flyers at the Spectrum?

Q7   How many times did the Flyers finish first in their division between 1967–68 and 1992–93?

Q8   During the Flyers' inaugural season, the club competed in the first NHL regular-season games ever played in five different arenas. Name the rinks that were the site of these milestone games.

Q9   On October 11, 1967, the Flyers went down to defeat in their first-ever game. What team ruined the Flyers' debut by a 5–1 score?

Q10   Exactly one week later, the Flyers earned the team's first win, 2–1, in their opponent's rink. What club did the Flyers edge on October 18, 1967?

Q11   Thanks to a goal off the stick of Bill Sutherland, the Flyers eked out a 1–0 win over the Penguins in Philly's first-ever game at the Spectrum. Which Flyer goalie recorded the shutout?

Q12   Who scored the first goal in Spectrum history?

Q13   One of the worst stick fights in the history of the NHL took place during a game between the Boston Bruins and Flyers on March 7, 1968. Name the players who faced off in the stick-swinging match.

Q14   Whose original idea was it to play a recording of Kate Smith's "God Bless America" in place of the National Anthem prior to Flyers' home games?

PHILADELPHIA FLYERS

A1   (A) 3
(B) 2
(C) 1
(D) 4

A2   Montreal Canadiens
New York Rangers
Boston Bruins
Chicago Black Hawks
Toronto Maple Leafs
Detroit Red Wings

A3   L.A. Kings
St. Louis Blues
Minnesota North Stars
Pittsburgh Penguins
Oakland Seals

A4   Wayne Connelly (January 10, 1967: at Minnesota)

A5   Buffalo's Rick Martin (January 31, 1971: at the Spectrum against Bernie Parent)

A6   New York Islanders (November 8, 1975: 4–3)
Boston Bruins (December 28, 1975: 4–2)

A7   10 (1967–68, 1973/74, 1974/75, 1975/76, 1976/77, 1979/80, 1982/83, 1984/85, 1985/86, 1986/87)

A8   Oakland/Alameda County Coliseum Arena
L.A. Forum
New Madison Square Garden
The Spectrum
Quebec City's Le Colisee

A9   California Seals (in Oakland)

A10   St. Louis Blues

A11   Doug Favell

A12   Flyer Bill "Sudsy" Sutherland

A13   Flyer Larry Zeidel engaged Eddie Shack

A14   Flyer vice president Lou Scheinfeld's

Q15   Kate Smith made her first personal appearance in the Spectrum on October 11, 1973. What club did Philadelphia defeat that evening, 2–0?

Q16   Kate Smith made three live appearances in the Spectrum, which resulted in three Flyer victories. Against what clubs did Smith work her miracle?

Q17   The Flyers have won more games than any other NHL expansion team (post-1966–67). Who ranks second to Philadelphia?

Q18   Who was the first Flyer to appear in an All-Star Game?

Q19   Who was the first Flyer to score a goal in an NHL All-Star Game?

Q20   Who was the first Flyer defenseman to be named to an NHL first all-star team?

Q21   Name the three Flyer rookies who participated in the 1979–80 All-Star Game.

Q22   What opposing player once registered six assists in a game against the Flyers?

Q23   Who was the Flyers' representative to the 1992 All-Star Game?

Q24   Prior to the 1992 All-Star Game in Philadelphia, the Coca-Cola Classic All-Star Skills Competition was held. Match the category with the winner.
(A) Hardest Shot   (1) Ray Bourque
(B) Fastest Skater   (2) Mike Richter
(C) Accuracy Shooting   (3) Al MacInnis
(D) Goaltender   (4) Sergei Fedorov

Q25   Philadelphia hosted the 1992 All-Star Game and saw the Campbell Conference defeat the Wales Conference 10–6. Who was selected MVP of the contest?

Q26   Who was the first recipient of the Bobby Clarke Trophy (Flyers' MVP)?

Q27   The Frank Selke Award is given each year by the Professional Hockey Writers' Association to "the forward who best excels in the defensive aspects of the game." Name the two Flyers who have been accorded this honor.

Q28   On March 13, 1993, the "storm of the century" rocked the East Coast. The Flyers were playing an afternoon game when the high winds caused the corridor windows of the Spectrum to blow out. Who were the Flyers playing on that unusual day?

PHILADELPHIA FLYERS

A15   Toronto Maple Leafs (Doug Favell was in goal for Toronto that evening.)

A16   Toronto (October 11, 1973: 2–0 win)
Boston (May 19, 1974: 1–0 win)
N.Y. Islanders (May 13, 1975: 4–1 win)

A17   Buffalo Sabres

A18   Leon Bochefort (January 16, 1968)

A19   Simon Nolet (1971–72)

A20   Mark Howe (1982/83)

A21   Pete Peeters
Brian Propp
Norm Barnes

A22   Penguin Ron Stackhouse (March 8, 1975)

A23   Rod Brind'Amour

A24   (A) 3
(B) 4
(C) 1
(D) 2

A25   Brett Hull (two goals and an assist)

A26   Pelle Lindbergh (April 4, 1985)

A27   Bobby Clarke (1983)
Dave Poulin (1987)

A28   Los Angeles Kings

SETTING THE STANDARDS

Q1 The 1975–76 Flyers tied a league record set 46 years earlier when they won 20 straight regular-season games at home. Whose mark did they equal?

Q2 Who set an NHL record during the 1981–82 season when he played in 83 regular-season games?

Q3 What is the team record for consecutive games without being shut out?

Q4 What club handled Philadelphia its worst loss?

Q5 What club did Philadelphia defeat a club-record 23 straight games at the Spectrum?

Q6 What are the most road games that the Flyers have won in a season?

Q7 The Flyers went four seasons before they registered a victory in their season opener in 1970–71. Who did they defeat for that win?

Q8 What is the longest losing streak endured by the Flyers?

Q9 The Flyers once lost nine consecutive games against a club in the Spectrum. What team dominated Philly on their home turf?

Q10 Of the 40 home games played by the 1975–76 Flyers, they only lost two. What is the only NHL club to lose fewer home games in an 80–game season?

Q11 The 1979–80 Flyers established an NHL record for the longest undefeated streak in a season. How many games did they go without a loss?

Q12 Who ended the Flyers' NHL record streak for the most games without a loss?

Q13 Who holds the club record for victories by a rookie netminder?

Q14 This Flyer goalie played in one game for six minutes and surrendered one goal, for a 10.00 goals-against average—an all-time club high. Name him.

Q15 Pete Peeters set an NHL record for rookie goalies with a 27-game undefeated streak (22–0–5) during the 1979–80 season. He also ranks second among all-time goalies with the streak. Who is the only NHL goalie to be ahead of the Flyer netminder?

Q16 Name the club that defeated the Flyers on February 19, 1980, and ended Pete Peeters's stretch of 27 games without a defeat.

PHILADELPHIA FLYERS

A1   Boston Bruins (1929–30)

A2   Brad Marsh (He played in 17 games with Calgary and 66 games with the Flyers.)

A3   120 (December 28, 1984 through March 27, 1986)

A4   Chicago Black Hawks (January 30, 1969: 12–0)

A5   Pittsburgh Penguins (February 19, 1980 through February 19, 1987)

A6   22 (1973–74)

A7   Minnesota North Stars (2–1 at the Spectrum)

A8   Six games (March 25, 1970 through April 4, 1970)

A9   Boston Bruins (November 21, 1970 through February 15, 1973)

A10   Montreal Canadiens (1976–77: 1 game)

A11   35 games (25 wins, 10 ties)

A12   Minnesota North Stars (January 7, 1980: 7–1 at Minneapolis)

A13   Ron Hextall (1986–87: 37 wins)

A14   Jerome Mrazek (1975–76)

A15   Boston's Gerry Cheevers (1971–72: 32 games)

A16   Colorado Rockies

*** FAST FACTS ***

The 1973–74 Philadelphia Flyers were the first expansion club to win the Stanley Cup.

Pelle Lindbergh was a member of Sweden's Bronze Medal Olympic team in 1980. He was the only netminder to earn a tie against the U.S. Gold Medal team that year.

Q17 Who scored the 5,000th goal in Flyer history?

Q18 The Flyers have defeated an opponent by 11 goals twice in their history. Name the clubs.

Q19 Philadelphia has won by a seven-goal margin while on the road in three different instances. Name the home teams in those games.

Q20 Who was the first Flyer to have back-to-back two-goal games?

Q21 Name the Flyer trio who set an NHL record for a line when they netted a combined total of 141 goals during the 1975–76 season.

Q22 What Flyer established an NHL record when he became the youngest player (23 years old) to net 50 goals in a season?

Q23 Who was the first Flyer to net 50 goals in a season?

Q24 Who holds the Philadelphia record for the fastest two goals (8 seconds) by one player?

Q25 In the 1967–68 season, the Flyers had two skaters net 20 goals. Name the Philly pair.

Q26 Tim Kerr set an NHL record when he netted 34 power-play goals in the 1985–86 season. Name the pair who held the old league mark of 28 power-play goals in a year.

Q27 Who holds the NHL playoff record for the fastest four goals in a postseason game?

Q28 In February 1982, Ron Flockhart shattered a club record when he scored a goal in eight consecutive games. Who held the team mark prior to Flockhart?

Q29 Only two Flyers have 10 or more hat tricks in their career. Name them.

Q30 Who was the opposing player who netted six goals in a game against the Flyers?

Q31 Name the three Flyers who once netted three goals within 35 seconds of each other—a team record.

Q32 The Flyers have netted three shorthanded goals in a game on two different occasions. Name the clubs Philly scored against.

PHILADELPHIA FLYERS

A17   Ron Sutter (March 16, 1985: at Toronto; the first-period goal came during a 6–1 victory against the Maple Leafs.)

A18   Pittsburgh Penguins (10/20/77: 11–0 at the Spectrum)
Vancouver Canucks (10/18/84: 13–2 at the Spectrum)

A19   California Seals (2/25/73: 7–0)
Minnesota North Stars (3/5/75: 9–2)
Washington Capitals (1/4/81: 8–1)

A20   Dick Sarrazin (12/15/68: at New York Rangers, won 3–1;
12/17/68: vs. Pittsburgh, won 8–2)

A21   Bobby Clarke (30 goals)
Reggie Leach (61 goals)
Bill Barber (50 goals)

A22   Rick MacLeish (1972–73)

A23   Rick MacLeish (April 1, 1973; vs. Pittsburgh)

A24   Ron Flockhart (December 6, 1981: vs. St. Louis Blues)

A25   Leon Rochefort (21)
Bill Sutherland (20)

A26   Bruin Phil Esposito (1971–72)
Islander Mike Bossy (1980–81)

A27   Tim Kerr (4/13/85: 8:16 at New York Rangers)

A28   Gary Dornhoefer (seven consecutive games)

A29   Tim Kerr (17)
Rick MacLeish (12)

A30   St. Louis's Red Berenson (11/7/68)

A31   Behn Wilson
Blake Dunlop
Al Hill
(3/1/79: vs. Boston)

A32   Washington Capitals (12/15/84)
Calgary Flames (1/13/85)

SETTING THE STANDARD

Q33 The Flyers twice scored 13 goals in a game. Who were the club's patsies those evenings?

Q34 Four goals in 1 minute, 22 seconds, a Flyer record, were scored against Pittsburgh on October 11, 1981. Name the four players involved in the scoring flurry.

Q35 What are the most goals tallied by the Flyers in a season-opening game?

Q36 Who scored the fastest Philly goal to open a game?

Q37 Name the two Flyers who have netted seven shorthanded goals in a season.

Q38 Bobby Clarke leads the Flyers in three all-time categories—assists (852), points (1,210), and games (1,144)—but ranks only fourth in goals (358). Name the three Flyers ahead of Clarke in this category.

Q39 Other than Bobby Clarke, no Flyer has registered 100 points in a season. Who has come closest to the century plateau in single-season points?

Q40 Who is the Flyers' single-season record holder with 12 game-winning goals?

Q41 Who set a club record when he scored goals in nine consecutive games?

Q42 Philadelphia has been in five scoreless games. Name the four opponents in the 0–0 ties.

Q43 What are the most single-season goals tallied by the Flyers?

Q44 Five Flyers have scored four goals in a game (as of 1992). Name them.

Q45 Twice the Flyers have scored dual goals within seven seconds of each other. Name the Philly players involved in this record.

Q46 Who led the Flyers in penalty minutes for the 1967–68 season?

Q47 Only once in the club's history have the Flyers played a game without having a penalty called against them. What team were they facing that evening?

Q48 Only once in the history of the club has a Flyer led the team in penalty minutes without being penalized more than 100 minutes. Name the player with this distinction.

PHILADELPHIA FLYERS

A33   Pittsburgh Penguins (March 22, 1984: at the Spectrum)
          Vancouver Canucks (October 18, 1984: at the Spectrum)

A34   Bobby Clarke
          Ilkka Sinisalo
          Reggie Leach
          Ken Linseman

A35   Nine (1982–83 opener: vs. Quebec)

A36   Tim Kerr (3/7/89: 0:08 vs. Edmonton)

A37   Brian Propp (1984/85)
          Mark Howe (1985–86)

A38   Bill Barber (420)
          Brian Propp (369)
          Tim Kerr (363)

A39   Tim Kerr (1984–85: 98 points)

A40   Brian Propp (1982–83)

A41   Rich Tocchet (3/1/89 to 3/19/89)

A42   Los Angeles (3/14/68)
          St. Louis (10/26/69)
          Pittsburgh (10/17/70, 12/4/82)
          New York Rangers (3/30/81)

A43   350 (1983–84)

A44   Rick MacLeish
          Tom Bladon
          Tim Kerr
          Brian Propp
          Rich Tocchet

A45   Dave Brown and Brian Propp (12/2/86: vs. St. Louis)
          Moe Mantha and Ron Sutter (12/27/88: vs. Washington)

A46   Ed Van Impe (141)

A47   St. Louis Blues (3/18/79)

A48   Gary Dornhoefer (1970–71: 93 minutes)

Q49   Who is the Flyers' all-time penalty-minute leader?

Q50   Dave Schultz set a club (and NHL) record with 472 penalty minutes in the 1974–75 season. Who holds the Flyers' single-season record for penalty minutes among defensemen?

Q51   What opposing player set an NHL record for penalty minutes in a game against the Flyers on March 11, 1979?

Q52   Who was the first Flyer defenseman to attempt a penalty shot?

Q53   Who scored the first goal on a penalty shot in Flyer history?

Q54   Who took the first penalty shot in Flyer history?

Q55   Who was the first Flyer to crack the NHL's top 10 scoring list for a season?

Q56   Tom Bladon registered eight points in one game, the most ever by an NHL defenseman, in a home game on December 11, 1977. Against what club were the Flyers playing that evening?

Q57   Name the Flyer who set an NHL record in 1977 for points by a player in his first NHL game.

Q58   Who holds the club single-season record for points by a center?

Q59   Who holds the club single-season record for points by a rookie?

Q60   Marke Howe is the Flyers' all-time point leader among defensemen, with 480 points. Who ranks second, with 230 points?

Q61   Who holds the club single-season record for points by a left wing?

Q62   Who holds the club single-season record for points by a defenseman?

Q63   Who holds the club single-season record for points by a right wing?

Q64   What team once took 55 shots against the Flyers, the most allowed in Philadelphia's history?

Q65   What are the most shots on goal that the Flyers have taken in one game?

PHILADELPHIA FLYERS

A49   Rich Tocchet (1,683)

A50   Glen Cochrane (1981–82: 329 minutes)

A51   Randy Holt (While playing for the L.A. Kings, he accumulated 67 minutes.)

A52   Behn Wilson (12/17/81: vs. Buffalo's Don Edwards; he scored.)

A53   Orest Kindrachuk (11/9/74: vs. Washington's Michel Belhumeur)

A54   Bill Clement (3/7/73: vs. Detroit's Jim Rutherford; the attempt was unsuccessful.)

A55   Bobby Clarke (He finished 10th that year with 81 points.)

A56   Cleveland Barons (The Flyers won 11–1 as Bladon scored four goals and had four assists in the contest.)

A57   Al Hill (February 14, 1977: two goals, three assists for five points vs. St. Louis at the Spectrum)

A58   Bobby Clarke (1975–76: 30 goals, 89 assists: 119 points)

A59   Dave Poulin (1983–84: 31 goals, 45 assists: 76 points)

A60   Tom Bladon

A61   Bill Barber (1975–76: 50 goals, 62 assists: 112 points)

A62   Mark Howe (1985–86: 24 goals, 58 assists: 82 points)

A63   Tim Kerr (1984–85: 54 goals, 44 assists: 98 points)

A64   Montreal Canadiens (January 3, 1977)

A65   62 (April 1, 1976: vs. Washington at the Spectrum)

GLORY DAYS

Q1   Name the Flyer goalie who lost the only playoff game he ever played in.

Q2   Bernie Parent is the winningest netminder in Flyer postseason play with a 232–141–103 record, but he does not have the best winning percentage. Who leads the club with an overall record of 3–0–1 and .875 percentage?

Q3   Which Flyer has scored 10 game-winning goals in the postseason?

Q4   Name the two Flyers who have netted 53 goals in postseason play.

Q5   In Game 6 of the 1987 finals, the Flyers' winning goal was scored with only 5:32 to play. Who netted the winner against Edmonton?

Q6   The Flyers won their division in the first year of their existence. What was the name of the Western Division title they claimed?

Q7   The Flyers won the Western Division in the first year of their existence. What club did they meet in the playoffs?

Q8   What Flyer registered a hat trick during the 1968 playoffs?

Q9   The leading scorers for the Flyers in the 1968 playoffs registered a mere five points over the seven-game series. Who were they?

Q10   Who scored the game-winner in the April 16, 1968 quarterfinal game against the Blues?

Q11   The Flyers needed a victory in the last game of the 1970 season in order to make the playoffs. They lost the final contest 1–0 when Bernie Parent lost sight of the puck in the sun, which was shining through a Spectrum exit. Name the Minnesota player who scored on the blinding shot.

Q12   The Flyers needed only a tie in the last game of the 1971–72 season to enter the playoffs, but a goal with four seconds left sent Philly packing. Name the Sabre who won the game for Buffalo and killed the club's postseason hopes.

Q13   During the 1974 June expansion and intraleague drafts, the Flyers only lost one player from its championship club. Who was he?

Q14   When Philly won the second game of the 1974 Stanley Cup Series, the team broke a string of losses at the Boston Garden. When was the last time the Flyers had won in Beantown previous to their overtime victory on May 9, 1974?

Q15   The Flyers evened the 1974 Stanley Cup Finals series at 1–1 with a 3–2 victory on May 9, 1974. Who scored the overtime goal for Philadelphia?

PHILADELPHIA FLYERS

A1   Dunc Wilson (1970)

A2   Gary Inness

A3   Rick MacLeish

A4   Bill Barber
          Rick MacLeish

A5   J. J. Daigneault

A6   The Campbell Bowl

A7   St. Louis Blues (The Blues won the best-of-seven playoff, 4–3.)

A8   Rosaire Paiement (April 13, 1968)

A9   Andre Lacroix (2 goals, 3 assists)
          Forbes Kennedy (1 goal, 4 assists)

A10   Don Blackburn (11:18 of the second overtime period)

A11   Barry Gibbs

A12   Gerry Mehan

A13   Simon Nolet

A14   November 12, 1967 (4 years, 5 months, 27 days—19 games without a win)

A15   Bobby Clarke

*** FAST FACTS ***

SPECTRUM ICE STATS —
Rink Size: 200 × 85 feet
Paint: 60 gallons white
3 gallons red
2 gallons blue
Piping: 12 miles (for ice)
Water needed: 3,000 gallons
Thickness: 1 inch
Boards: 52 sections
Glass: 208 panes

Q16 Who did Philadelphia sweep in the 1974 Stanley Cup Quarterfinals?

Q17 In Game 3 of the 1974 Stanley Cup Finals, Gary Dornhoefer suffered a separated shoulder that knocked him out of the rest of the playoffs. What Bruin laid the hit on Dorny?

Q18 Who was the highest scorer for the Flyers in the 1973–74 Stanley Cup playoffs?

Q19 Rick MacLeish netted the game- and Cup-winner in Game 6 of the 1974 finals against Boston. Whose shot did he tip in?

Q20 The first game of the 1975 quarterfinals with Toronto went into overtime with the score tied 3–3. Who put the winner in the net at 1:45 of the OT period?

Q21 With Philadelphia down 3–2 in the 1975 semifinals, Game 6 went into overtime with the score tied at 4–4. Who slapped the winner into the Islanders' goal at 2:56 of the overtime period?

Q22 Who scored the game-winning goal in Game 6 of the 1975 Stanley Cup Finals?

Q23 Reggie Leach set an NHL record during the 1976 playoffs for the longest consecutive goal-scoring streak in a playoff year. How many games does it stretch?

Q24 What player tied an NHL playoff record by scoring five goals in a game during the 1976 quarterfinals?

Q25 It took only 23 seconds of the overtime period for the Flyers to be victorious over the Rockies in Game 1 of the preliminary round in the 1978 playoffs. Who netted the winner?

Q26 Bill Barber set an NHL record for shorthanded goals in a series during the 1980 semifinals against Minnesota. How many did he net?

Q27 The first Stanley Cup hat trick scored by a U.S.-born player was tallied in the 1980 finals. Name the Yank who netted the trio.

Q28 What two NHL records did Tim Kerr set in the third game of the 1985 division semifinal?

Q29 The Flyers won the 1984–85 Wales Conference Championship in six games over the Quebec Nordiques. Who scored a goal in the sixth game for Philadelphia while the Flyers were two men short?

PHILADELPHIA FLYERS

A16 Atlanta Flames

A17 Don Marcotte

A18 Rick MacLeish (13 goals, 9 assists: 22 points)

A19 Andre Dupont's

A20 Andre Dupont

A21 Bobby Clarke

A22 Bob Kelly

A23 Nine

A24 Darryl Sittler (April 22, 1976: Toronto won, 8–5.)

A25 Mel Bridgeman

A26 Three

A27 Paul Holmgren

A28 Most goals in one period (four goals, second period)
Fastest four goals by one player (8:16) (April 13, 1985: Flyers
won the game 6–5 and the series 3–0 from the Rangers.)

A29 Dave Poulin (The Flyers won the game 3–0.)

TRADES, WAIVES, AND ACQUISITIONS

Q1 In the 1967 expansion draft, the Flyers selected four players from the Bruin organization—the most from any club. Name the quartet chosen from Beantown.

Q2 Who were the first two players taken by the Flyers in the June 1967 draft?

Q3 Who did the Flyers choose with their first pick in the 1967 Amateur Draft?

Q4 Who was the first non-goalie selected by the Flyers in the 1967 expansion draft?

Q5 Defenseman Wayne Hillman came from Minnesota in a 1969 trade. Who was sent to the North Stars?

Q6 The Flyers dispatched two players to the Rangers in 1969 and received one in return. Who did Philly obtain in the swap?

Q7 Philly picked up Brent Hughes in a 1970 trade with Los Angeles. Who was sent to the West Coast in the deal?

Q8 What club traded Barry Ashbee to the Flyers in 1970?

Q9 What twosome came to Philadelphia in exchange for Bernie Parent and a draft pick in a 1971 deal with Toronto?

Q10 Who did Philly give up to L.A. in the 1971 trade that brought Larry Mickey to the City of Brotherly Love?

Q11 In 1971, the Flyers had two first-round picks in the Amateur Draft. Who did they select with the choices?

Q12 The Flyers were wheeling and dealing when they dispatched Mike Walton to Boston for Danny Schock and this All-Star. Who else came to the Flyers from Beantown in the 1971 trade?

Q13 Andre Dupont was acquired by the Flyers in 1972 from the Blues. What two players were given up to acquire "Moose"?

Q14 Name the four players acquired by the Flyers from Los Angeles in return for Bill Lesuk, Serge Bernier, Larry Brown, and Jimmy Johnson in a 1972 swap with the Kings.

Q15 In a 1973 late-season deal, the Flyers sent Jean Potvin and Glenn Irwin to the Islanders for one player. Who came down the pike to Philadelphia?

PHILADELPHIA FLYERS

A1   Bernie Parent
Joe Watson
Doug Favell
Gary Dornhoefer

A2   Bernie Parent
Doug Favell

A3   Serge Bernier

A4   Ed Van Impe (He was the third player selected by Philadelphia.)

A5   John Miszuk

A6   Reg Fleming

A7   Mike Byers

A8   Hershey Bears (of the American Hockey League)

A9   Bruce Gamble
Mike Walton

A10   Larry Hillman

A11   Larry Wright
Pierre Plante

A12   Rick MacLeish

A13   Brent Hughes
Pierre Plante

A14   Ross Lonsberry
Jean Potvin
Ed Joyal
Bill Flett

A15   Terry Crisp

TRADES, WAIVES, AND ACQUISITIONS

Q16   Mel Bridgeman was selected with the first overall pick in the 1975 draft. What did the Flyers give to the Capitals so that they could choose the center?

Q17   The Flyers had to send two players to the Penguins in order to acquire Gary Inness in 1976. Who did they sacrifice for the goalie?

Q18   The Flyers gave up Mark Suzor in the summer of 1977 to acquire Barry Dean. With what club did Philadelphia transact the deal?

Q19   In a January 20, 1977 trade with Vancouver, the Flyers sent Jack McIlhargey and Larry Goodenough to the Canucks. What player did they acquire?

Q20   What two players were traded to St. Louis in 1979 to acquire goalie Phil Myre?

Q21   Who did Philadelphia receive when they traded Mel Bridgeman to Calgary in 1981?

Q22   Rick MacLeish, Don Gillen, Blake Wesley, and the club's first-, second- and third-round picks in the 1982 draft were sent to Hartford in 1981. The Flyers received the Whalers' 1982 picks in the first and third rounds, as well as what two players?

Q23   Who did Philadelphia choose with the two Whaler picks they acquired in the 1982 draft?

Q24   On August 19, 1982, the Flyers obtained Mark Howe and a third-round choice in the 1983 draft from Hartford. Who did Philadelphia take with the draft selection?

Q25   Pete Peeters was traded to the Bruins in June 1982. What Boston player came to Philly in the deal?

Q26   The Flyers gave up two players and two 1982 draft picks (in the first and third rounds) to obtain Mark Howe from the Hartford Whalers in that August 1982 trade. Who did Philly give up in the deal?

Q27   Doug Crossman came to Philadelphia in a June 8, 1983 trade with Chicago. Who was sent to the Windy City?

Q28   What three players were sent to Pittsburgh so that the Flyers could acquire Rich Sutter?

Q29   Paul Holmgren was traded to the North Stars in February 1984. Name the player who came to Philly in the trade.

PHILADELPHIA FLYERS

A16   Bill Clement
Don McLean
Philadelphia's first-round pick (18th choice overall)

A17   Ed Van Impe
Bobby Taylor

A18   Colorado Rockies

A19   Bob Dailey

A20   Rick LaPointe
Blake Dunlop

A21   Brad Marsh

A22   Ray Allison
Fred Arthur

A23   First-round choice: Ron Sutter
Third-round choice: Miroslav Dvorak

A24   Derrick Smith

A25   Brad McCrimmon

A26   Ken Linseman
Greg Adams

A27   Behn Wilson

A28   Ron Flockhart
Mark Taylor
Andy Brickley

A29   Paul Guay

TRADES, WAIVES, AND ACQUISITIONS

Q30   The Flyers picked up Jean-Jacques Daigneault and two draft picks from the Canucks in a 1986 trade. What two players were sent to Vancouver in the transaction?

Q31   On December 18, 1986, the Flyers sent Bob Froese to the New York Rangers for a second-round pick in the 1989 draft and what player?

Q32   Name the player the Flyers sent to Quebec in 1988 in order to obtain defenseman Terry Carkner.

Q33   Mike Bullard came to the Flyers on November 29, 1988, in a deal with St. Louis. Who did the Blues receive for the center?

Q34   Jay Wells arrived from Los Angeles in a September 1988 trade. Who did the Flyers give up for the defenseman?

Q35   In February 1989, Keith Acton came to Philadelphia from Edmonton. Who did the Flyers give up in the trade with the Oilers?

Q36   Who did the Flyers send to Toronto on July 26, 1991, for "future considerations"?

Q37   On May 30, 1991, the Flyers picked up Dave Brown and Corey Foster, along with the rights to Jari Kurri, from Edmonton. Name the three players Philadelphia had to give up in the trade.

Q38   The Flyers picked up Steve Kasper and Steve Duchesne and a fourth-round pick in the 1991 Entry Draft from the Kings on May 30, 1991. What did they give up in the deal?

Q39   What did the Flyers gain when they sent Gord Murphy, Brian Dobbin, and the club's third-round pick in the 1992 Entry Draft to the Bruins?

PHILADELPHIA FLYERS

A30 Rich Sutter
Dave Richter
(and a 1986 third-round draft pick)

A31 Kjell Samuelsson

A32 Greg Smyth

A33 Peter Zezel

A34 Doug Crossman

A35 Dave Brown

A36 Mike Bullard

A37 Scott Mellanby
Craig Berube
Craig Fisher

A38 Jeff Chychrun
The rights to Jari Kurri.

A39 Garry Galley
Wes Walz
(plus future considerations)

Philadelphia Eagles

PHILADELPHIA EAGLES

PHILADELPHIA EAGLES
1960 National Football League Champions

Front Row: (L-R): Bobby Freeman, DB; Gene Johnson, DB; Ted Dean, FB; Billy Barnes, HB; Theron Sapp, FB; Bobby Jackson, DB; Norm Van Brocklin, QB; Buck Shaw, Head Coach; Sonny Jurgensen, QB; Clarence Peaks, FB; Timmy Brown, HB; Pete Retzlaff, E; Bobby Walston, E; Gerry Huth, G; Jerry Reichow, QB-E.

Middle Row: Chuck Weber, LB; Jimmy Carr, DB; Howard Keys, t; Riley Gunnels, DT; Jim McCusker, T; Stan Campbell, G; Marion Campbell, DE; Jesse Richardson, DT; Bob Pellegrini, LB; Bill Lapham, C; Gene Gossage, DE; Charlie Gauer, Asst. Coach; Jerry Williams, Asst. Coach; Nick Skorich, Asst. Coach; Ed Hogan, Pub. Dir.

Back Row: Maxie Baughan, LB; John Wittenborn, G; Dick Lucas, E; John Wilcox, DT; J. D. Smith, T; Ed Khayat, DT; Joe Robb, DE; Don Burroughs, DB; Tommy McDonald, FL; Tom Brookshier, DB; Chuck Bednarik, LB-C; John Nocera, LB; Tom McCoy, Trainer; Fred Schubach, Equip. Mgr.

THE SUITS

Q1   Which Eagle coach played pro football in Canton, Ohio, under an assumed name?

Q2   What onetime Eagle coach was a defensive stalwart on Philly's 1960 championship squad?

Q3   What Eagle coach was known as the "Silver Fox"?

Q4   Who succeeded Bert Bell as NFL commissioner when Bell died in 1960?

Q5   The Eagles' first coach compiled a 9–21–1 record during his three-year tenure, 1933–35. Who was the team's first skipper?

Q6   In 1935, this Eagle honcho came up with a proposal to use a college draft so that talent would be equally distributed throughout the league. Who was this innovative GM?

Q7   With whom did Art Rooney swap franchises in 1941 so he could return to Pittsburgh?

Q8   In 1946 owner Alexis Thompson opened the NFL's first permanent preseason training site. What was the camp called?

Q9   What was Greasy Neale's given name?

Q10   Greasy Neale played professional baseball as well as pro football. What club did the all-round athlete play with in the 1919 World Series?

Q11   Greasy Neale batted .357 in the 1919 World Series and was his victorious club's leading hitter. Why is this distinguished accomplishment somewhat tainted?

PHILADELPHIA EAGLES

A1   Greasy Neale

A2   Marion Campbell

A3   Buck Shaw

A4   Pete Rozelle

A5   Lud Wray

A6   Bert Bell

A7   Alexis Thompson

A8   "The Eagle's Nest"

A9   Earle

A10   Cincinnati Reds

A11   The 1919 Series involved the "Black Sox" scandal, in which eight Chicago White Sox players were accused of throwing the fall classic in favor of the underdog Reds.

*** FAST FACTS ***

Steeler head coach Bill Cowher, who played linebacker for the Eagles in 1983 and '84, is married to a former player from the Women's Professional Basketball League.

Steve Van Buren was turned down for football as a high school sophomore because he weighed only 125 pounds. He took two years off and worked in an iron foundry. Upon his return to school, he earned a scholarship to LSU, and even though he wasn't well-known the Eagles drafted him in the first round of the 1944 draft.

Although he was a star athlete at Cohen High in New Orleans, Roynell Young received only one firm scholarship offer as a senior. He accepted and went on to a stellar career at Alcorn State.

Which hat should he wear? "Greasy" Neale is a member of the Pro Football Hall of Fame, but his skills weren't limited to the gridiron. He is the only man to play in a World Series, coach a football team in the Rose Bowl, and snare an NFL title, two in 10 years with the Eagles.

Q12   Because of the merging of the Philadelphia and Pittsburgh franchises in 1943, the club had two head coaches. Who shared the reins of the team?

Q13   After 11 years at the helm, Greasy Neale was given the gate in 1951. His successor was the coach and GM of the Detroit Lions. Who was he?

Q14   In 1957 Frank McNamee took over as team president. McNamee also held a high-ranking post for the city of Philadelphia. What was that job?

Q15   After the Eagles were grounded by two straight losing seasons, head coach Nick Skorich was replaced in 1964 by Joe Kuharich. What league position was Kuharich holding when he was tapped as the Philly bench general?

Q16   Joe Kuharich signed a 15-year agreement as coach and general manager of the Eagles in 1964. How long did he last with the club?

Q17   Joe Kuharich left the Redskins' coaching post in 1958 to accept a similar position at the collegiate level. What school did he go to?

Q18   Following the death of James Clark in 1962, this businessman purchased the struggling Eagles for $5.5 million. Name the man who made his fortune in the building industry.

Q19   After Leonard Tose purchased the team for $16 million in 1969, he hired a former Eagle standout as his general manager. Who was he?

Q20   In 1971, Leonard Tose donated $79,000 to save a worthy program in the Philadelphia area. Who benefited from his act of charity?

Q21   When Leonard Tose purchased the team for a then-record $16.1 million, he installed two former Eagles as general manager and head coach. Who was that powerful tandem?

Q22   This Mississippi native took over the Eagles' coaching reins three games into the 1971 season. He lasted just one season in the top job. Who was he?

Q23   With what team did Mike McCormack establish himself as one of the greatest offensive linemen?

Q24   Which team drafted Kansas's Mike McCormack with its first-round pick in the 1951 draft?

Q25   In late 1974, Leonard Tose appointed assistant Jim Murray team general manager. Why was his promotion noteworthy?

PHILADELPHIA EAGLES

A12   Greasy Neale
Walt Kiesling

A13   Bo McMillin (Illness forced him to step down early in the season; his successor, Wayne Millner, also resigned because of ill health.)

A14   Fire commissioner

A15   He was chief of officials.

A16   Five years

A17   Notre Dame

A18   Jerry Wolman

A19   Pete Retzlaff

A20   The Philadelphia public school system (Tose's largess enabled the varsity football program to continue in the district.)

A21   GM Pete Retzlaff
Coach Jerry Williams

A22   Eddie Khayat

A23   Cleveland Browns

A24   New York Yanks

A25   At age 36, Murray was the youngest general manager in the NFL.

Q26 Who did Dick Vermeil's UCLA Bruins upset in the 1976 Rose Bowl by a 23–10 count?

Q27 Dick Vermeil had coaching experience as an assistant with only one other NFL club before taking the Eagles' top job in 1976. With what team was Vermeil an aide?

Q28 Dick Vermeil took the Eagles' helm in 1976. In what year was he honored as Coach of the Year?

Q29 True or false—Dick Vermeil ended up with less than a .500 winning mark as Eagle head coach.

Q30 Which Eagle major domo was voted Man of the Year in 1980 by the *Football News?*

Q31 Francis Marion Campbell was an All-Southeastern Conference tackle at the University of Georgia. He acquired his colorful nickname while attending that school. By what name was Campbell known?

Q32 After Marion Campbell was given the gate, this man took over as interim head coach for the final game of the 1985 season. Name him.

Q33 During Ronald Reagan's first term in the Oval Office, Norman Braman was tapped for a position in the administration. What post did the president offer?

Q34 On what three Super Bowl teams did Buddy Ryan serve as an assistant coach?

Q35 In what subject does Buddy Ryan have a master's degree from Middle Tennessee?

Q36 At what school was Rich Kotite the heavyweight boxing champion?

Q37 With what two teams did Rich Kotite earn a reputation as a hard-nosed tight end and special teams player?

Q38 What organization recognized the Kotite clan as the 1992 Family of the Year?

PHILADELPHIA EAGLES

A26 Ohio State

A27 Los Angeles Rams

A28 1978

A29 False. He compiled a 55–51–0 overall record.

A30 Leonard Tose

A31 "Swamp Fox"

A32 Fred Bruney

A33 Commissioner of U.S. Immigration and Naturalization Services (Braman declined the offer.)

A34 Chicago Bears (1985)
Minnesota Vikings (1976)
New York Jets (1968)

A35 Education

A36 University of Miami

A37 Giants (1967, 1969–72)
Steelers (1968)

A38 New York Catholic Archdiocese

Q1   After *Life* magazine ran an article entitled "Savagery on Sunday," two Eagles sued the magazine because they thought they were being unfairly portrayed. The players prevailed at the trial and were each awarded $25,000. Who were the two plaintiffs in the case?

Q2   This Eagle was the only player to be named to the All-NFL Team before the days of the two-platoon picks and then was named to both the offensive and defensive units after all-league choices were two-way. Identify this Hall of Famer.

Q3   An observer once said that this Eagle was three parts gorilla and one part Englishman. His life was cut short when he perished in a 1947 auto accident. Who was he?

Q4   What do Al Wistert, Walter Barnes, Chuck Bednarik, and Pete Pihos all have in common?

Q5   Name the pair of outstanding Birdmen who went, respectively, to Frankford High and Catholic High, as well as Temple.

Q6   Which Eagle kicker had the unusual first name of Loris?

Q7   At the age of 16, this Eagle was the youngest player ever to be invited twice to the Cincinnati Reds tryout camp. Who is this versatile athlete?

Q8   Which Eagle won the Arizona Gold Gloves boxing title at the age of 13?

Q9   Four Eagles have had the honor of being recognized as the MVP of the Pro Bowl. Identify the fab four.

Q10   Which pair of Eagle superstars, who played dual positions as center and linebacker, are enshrined in the Pro Football Hall of Fame?

Q11   This Hall of Famer toiled for both the Bears (1932–36) and Eagles (1937–39) and was the first player to be named to the NFL's all-league squad for two different teams. Who was he?

Q12   Which early-day Eagle star was known as "The Offside Kid" because of his quickness off the line?

Q13   In 1939, Bert Bell drafted a Texas Christian All-American quarterback with the club's first-round draft pick. Name the QB who demanded (and received) $12,000 per year plus a percentage of the gate for his services?

Q14   Which Eagle distinguished himself as an Air Force waist gunner and Air Medal winner during World War II?

PHILADELPHIA EAGLES

A1   Buck Kilroy
Wayne Robinson

A2   Pete Pihos

A3   Bill Hewitt

A4   They were the first Eagles voted to an All-Pro game (1951).

A5   Mike Jarmoluk (Frankford)
Bucko Kilroy (Catholic)

A6   Sam Baker

A7   Keith Byars

A8   Vai Sikahema

A9   Chuck Bednarik (1954)
Floyd Peters (1967)
Reggie White (1987)
Randall Cunningham (1989)

A10   Alex Wojciechowicz
Chuck Bednarik

A11   Bill Hewitt

A12   Bill Hewitt

A13   Davey O'Brien (The "superstar" lasted only two years in the NFL.)

A14   Chuck Bednarik

THE UNIFORMS

Q15   This all-purpose back was acquired by the Eagles for $100 from the Cleveland Rams in 1942. He was called the "Crooning Halfback" because he sang during halftime. Who was this unusual athlete?

Q16   In what round was Temple's Bucko Kilroy drafted by the Birds?

Q17   Bucko Kilroy earned his "ironman" status with the Eagles when he labored 13 years in a Philly uniform (1943–56). During Kilroy's first 12 seasons, how many games did he miss?

Q18   In what country not known for its football heritage was Steve Van Buren born?

Q19   In the same year that the Eagles fell to the Chicago Cardinals for the championship, Steve Van Buren etched his name in the record books as the first player to rush for 1,000 yards. In what year did these events occur?

Q20   During the course of Steve Van Buren's stellar career, he rushed for more than 1,000 yards twice, captured four league rushing titles, and in 1945 compiled a Triple Crown. What league-leading figures did Supersonic Steve's Triple Crown include?

Q21   What was the name of the Fordham line on which Alex Wojciechowicz first gained fame as a center?

Q22   What team picked Alex Wojciechowicz as the number one choice in the 1938 draft?

Q23   What Hall of Fame coach played alongside Alex Wojciechowicz on the Fordham defensive line?

Q24   Before this early-day Eagle QB entered West Philadelphia High, he was the team's mascot and water boy. Who was he?

Q25   By what nickname was Pete Pihos known?

Q26   What two positions did Pete Pihos play?

Q27   In what category did Pete Pihos lead the NFL for three straight seasons—1953, '54, and '55?

Q28   An All-American in football and a 1948 Olympian in track, this Eagle halfback was considered the fastest human of his time. Who was he?

Q29   How did the Eagles acquire Chuck Bednarik?

PHILADELPHIA EAGLES

A15 Bosh Pritchard (who also had his own radio show)

A16 He as never drafted; Kilroy made the team after asking for a tryout.

A17 One

A18 Honduras

A19 1947

A20 Rushing
Scoring
Kickoff returns

A21 The "Seven Blocks of Granite"

A22 Detroit Lions

A23 Vince Lombardi

A24 Bill Mackrides

A25 "The Golden Greek"

A26 End and fullback

A27 Pass-receiving

A28 Clyde Scott

A29 He was the team's 1949 bonus draft choice.

Q30   Besides his outstanding work as a center, linebacker, and kickoff special-ist, what disaster position did Chuck Bednarik play for the Eagles?

Q31   Besides their Philadelphia heritage, Mike Jarmoluk and Bucko Kilroy had something else in common: Neither man wore a standard piece of football equipment, because they believed it slowed them down. What did each player go without?

Q32   Which longtime NFL head coach was the Eagles' number one draft pick in 1950?

Q33   Who played in the Birds' "Elephant Backfield"?

Q34   Called the younger half of "Jim Clark's Moving Vans," Steve Van Buren's kid brother joined the Eagles in 1951 as a halfback-linebacker. The younger Van Buren was an LSU product and a Purple Heart recipient. What was his first name?

Q35   Despite having the left side of his face fractured in a 1953 game, this Eagle back missed only two games during the year. Who was this Philly tough guy?

Q36   Hall of Famer Chuck Bednarik was a member of the famed Suicide Seven of the mid-fifties. Who were the other players on that fearsome squad?

Q37   This present-day broadcaster won a starting role as a defensive back as a rookie in 1953, but his career was interrupted when he joined the air force. He served as an assistant coach at the academy two years later. Name him.

Q38   What team originally drafted Pete Retzlaff in the 22nd round of the draft, but then sold him to the Eagles for the $100 waiver fee before the 1956 game opener?

Q39   Who replaced Pete Retzlaff as the Eagles' tight end after the Baron retired in 1966?

Q40   Considered by some as Duke's greatest quarterback, this player was christened Christian Adolph. Identify him.

Q41   Which Philly receiver had his thumb and part of a finger shot off in a hunting accident when he was a child?

Q42   In 1961 the Dutchman was named head coach of a brand-new NFL franchise. What team did Norm Van Brocklin lead?

PHILADELPHIA EAGLES

A30 He was also the team's backup punter.

A31 Hip pads

A32 Bud Grant

A33 Toy Ledbetter
Dick Bielski
Jim Parmer

A34 Ebert

A35 Toy Ledbetter

A36 Norm Willey
Wayne Robinson
Mike Jarmoluk
Jess Richardson
Bucko Kilroy
Tom Scott

A37 Tom Brookshier (He rejoined the Birds in 1956.)

A38 Detroit Lions

A39 Mike Ditka

A40 Sonny Jurgensen

A41 Tommy McDonald

A42 Minnesota Vikings

THE UNIFORMS

Q43 Known as "Bomber," this Georgia product was picked as the school's Back of the Decade. Who was this standout runner?

Q44 In what other field did Eagle great Timmy Brown make a name for himself?

Q45 At the end of the championship season of 1960, two members of the Philadelphia organization called it quits. Who quite while the team was at the top?

Q46 Which Eagle snagged the John Wanamaker Award as Philadelphia's Outstanding Athlete of 1960?

Q47 Nicknamed the "Blade," this player was originally signed by the Rams as a quarterback. He joined the Eagles in 1960 and distinguished himself as a free safety. Who is he?

Q48 Who replaced Tom Brookshier at right corner after he hung up his cleats in 1961?

Q49 Name the free agent who succeeded Bobby Walston in 1963 as the Eagles' placekicker and kickoff man.

Q50 With the Eagles from 1964–73, this defensive end worked as a deputy sheriff in the off-season. Who was the man behind the badge?

Q51 When Ollie Matson joined the Eagles in 1964, it was the third time that his path had crossed that of Eagles head coach Joe Kuharich. Where had the two worked together before?

Q52 Besides his two-year stint with the Birds, with what other teams did Ollie Matson play in his illustrious 15-year NFL career?

Q53 This Eagle soared to the top of the team's rushing ranks for three consecutive seasons—1967, '68, and '69. Who was at the top of the club's rushing heap?

Q54 Which Eagle guard played four years in the Milwaukee Braves' farm system as an outfielder before turning to football in 1967?

Q55 Identify the pair of Birds who co-captained USC's 1967 national championship team.

Q56 This Eagle defensive star was a runner-up to O.J. Simpson in the 1969 Heisman Trophy balloting. Name the Purdue product.

Q57 At what position was Steve Zabel drafted from Oklahoma by the Eagles in 1970?

PHILADELPHIA EAGLES

A43   Theron Sapp

A44   Music (He sang on several records.)

A45   QB Norm Van Brocklin
Head coach Buck Shaw

A46   Chuck Bednarik

A47   Don Burroughs

A48   Irv Cross

A49   Michael Clark

A50   Don Hultz

A51   San Francisco College
Chicago Cardinals
(In both instances, Kuharich coached Matson.)

A52   Chicago Cardinals
Los Angeles Rams
Detroit Lions

A53   Tom Woodeshick

A54   Dick Hart

A55   Tim Rossovich
Adrian Young

A56   Leroy Keyes

A57   Tight end

Q58 Although Wade Key was the Eagles' first-round choice in the 1969 draft, he didn't join the team until the following season. Where did he play in the interim?

Q59 What is Harold Carmichael's given name?

Q60 Identify the quarterback who was the Canadian Football League's MVP in 1967 and as acquired by Philly from Denver for a draft choice in 1971.

Q61 Before coming to the Eagles in 1971, this player set an NFL record by kicking a 63-yard field goal. Who is this long-distance kicker?

Q62 Which defunct team made Norm Bulaich its number one pick in the 1970 draft?

Q63 Only one Eagle was tapped to play in the 1972 Pro Bowl. Who was so honored?

Q64 By what nickname was Ron James better known?

Q65 A 12th-round pick in 1973, this Eagle was believed to be the only NFL player to perform while wearing glasses. Name the man who made a spectacle of himself.

Q66 Identify the two players who were chosen ahead of Jerry Sisemore in the 1973 draft.

Q67 Which two Eagle quarterbacks attended New Hanover High School in North Carolina?

Q68 What NFL award did Roman Gabriel snare in 1973, the season he led the league in pass attempts, completions, and yardage?

Q69 Roman Gabriel probably had little trouble spotting his trio of "fire-high gang" receivers, three of the tallest players in the league during the mid-seventies. Who made up the gang?

Q70 How long did Frank LeMaster toil on the defensive line before he was chosen for a Pro Bowl slot?

Q71 Who replaced Frank LeMaster at right inside linebacker after the veteran was injured and traded to the 49ers in 1984?

Q72 Name the Eagle QB who tossed two touchdown passes to lead the NFC to a come-from-behind triumph in the 1975 Pro Bowl.

PHILADELPHIA EAGLES

A58   Key played on a minor league team, the Pottstown Firebirds.

A59   Lee

A60   Pete Liske

A61   Tom Dempsey

A62   Baltimore Colts

A63   Bill Bradley

A64   "Po"

A65   Joe Lavender

A66   John Matuszak (Houston)
Bert Jones (Baltimore)

A67   Roman Gabriel
Sonny Jurgensen

A68   Comeback Player of the Year

A69   Harold Carmichael (6′8″)
Charley Young (6′4″)
Don Zimmerman (6′4″)

A70   Seven years (He entered the NFL in 1974 and played in the Pro Bowl in 1981.)

A71   Anthony Griggs

A72   Mike Boryla (final score: 23–20)

Q73 Born in Dortumund, Germany, this Eagle kicker was a pro soccer player in Europe and the United States. He spent three years with the Birds and lived in his native country during the off-season. Who was he?

Q74 Even though he missed six and a half games because of injury, this rookie running back led the Eagles in rushing with 561 yards during the 1976 season. Who was this outstanding freshman?

Q75 Linebacker Terry Tautolo played for Dick Vermeil at UCLA in the early seventies. What unusual course of study did he major in?

Q76 Vince Papale never played college football, but he still made it to the pro ranks. With what club did he enter professional football in 1976?

Q77 How old was Vince Papale when he made his NFL debut with the Eagles in 1976?

Q78 A defensive end, this Vietnam vet made the Eagle squad as a 30-year-old rookie in 1977 and went on to lead the team with 10 sacks that season. Who had this unusual history?

Q79 A free agent acquisition in 1977, this Bird appeared in *Semi-Tough* and *Two-Minute Warning*. He joined the Eagles after his wife urged team scouts to watch his WFL tapes. Name this thespian-athlete.

Q80 In what Robin Williams movie did Herman Edwards appear?

Q81 What Eagle scooped up a Joe Pisarcik fumble and scampered 26 yards for a TD with 31 seconds left to propel the Birds to a 19–17 win over the Giants in the 1978 "Miracle of the Meadowlands"?

Q82 This player, whom scouts said "looked like Tarzan but played like Jane," proved the critics wrong when he won a spot on the defensive line in 1978. Who was he?

Q83 Dick Vermeil signed his nephew to a free agent contract in 1978. Name this durable running back.

Q84 Who took on the kicking duties after Nick Mike-Mayer was sidelined by injury with four games left in the 1978 season?

Q85 Claude Humphrey played 11 years in Atlanta before joining the Eagles in a 1979 trade for draft choices. What team picked the veteran end in the first round of the 1968 draft?

Q86 Jerry Robinson was a three-time consensus All-American. Who was the last collegiate player to be so honored for three consecutive years?

PHILADELPHIA EAGLES

A73   Horst Muhlmann

A74   Mike Hogan

A75   Kinesiology

A76   Philadelphia Bell (of the WFL)

A77   30 years old

A78   Lem Burnham

A79   Eric Johnson

A80   *The Best of Times*

A81   Herman Edwards

A82   Dennis Harrison

A83   Loie Giammona

A84   Punter Mike Michel

A85   Atlanta Falcons

A86   Doak Walker (1947–49)

*** FAST FACTS ***

EAGLES IN THE HALLOWED HALLS OF CANTON:

Bert Bell	Earl "Greasy" Neale
Steve Van Buren	Pete Pihos
Chuck Bednarik	Norm Van Brocklin
Alex Wojciechowicz	Bill Hewitt
Ollie Matson	Jim Ringo
Mike Ditka	Sonny Jurgensen

Ray Ellis overcame insurmountable odds when he made the team after he was the next-to-last player selected (331st overall) in the 1981 draft.

In spite of not playing football until his senior year in high school, Fred Barnett earned all-district honors and took the MVP award as a receiver-defensive back.

THE UNIFORMS

Q87   What former UCLA teammate did Jerry Robinson displace as the starting linebacker in the 1979 season?

Q88   For what U.S. senator did Yale alum John Spagnola serve as a driver in the pol's successful 1980 campaign?

Q89   Tony Franklin was the first kicker at his school to receive a full scholarship. What is Franklin's alma mater?

Q90   Tony Franklin was the first player in football history to kick two field goals longer than 60 yards in a game. For what college was Franklin playing when he achieved that feat in 1976?

Q91   Which Eagle snagged the Maxwell Football Club's Bert Bell Award as player of the year in 1980?

Q92   Who was named Mississippi's pro athlete of 1980?

Q93   Which Eagle won the NFL's Man of the Year award in 1980?

Q94   Before Joe Pisarcik joined the Eagles in 1980, he played for two other pro franchises. Name the teams.

Q95   Who were the two rookie free agents who appeared in all 16 regular-season games in 1981?

Q96   This Bird inked a free agent pact with the Eagles in 1981 after his line coach at Eastern Illinois met him in Washington, D.C., where he was working in construction. Who had this unusual entree into pro ball?

Q97   At what position was Leonard Mitchell originally drafted as the team's number one choice in 1981?

Q98   Who was the only Eagle selected to the Pro Bowl following the 1982 strike-shortened season?

Q99   With what name did Anthony Griggs and Vyto Kab christen their custom clothing company?

Q100   Name the baseball team that drafted Dan Pastorini as a pitcher out of high school.

Q101   What pair of cousins played on the same Eagle squad in the mid-eighties?

Q102   Which Eagle running back once worked as a barber in his father's shop?

PHILADELPHIA EAGLES

A87   Terry Tautolo

A88   Bill Bradley

A89   Texas A & M

A90   Texas A & M (64, 65 yards)

A91   Ron Jaworski

A92   Wilbert Montgomery

A93   Harold Carmichael

A94   Calgary (CFL)
New York Giants

A95   Greg Brown
Frank Giddens

A96   Greg Brown

A97   Defensive end

A98   Dennis Harrison

A99   TELB (which stood for their positions on the team, tight end and linebacker)

A100   New York Mets

A101   Elbert Foules
Wilbert Montgomery

A102   Major Everett

Q103 The Eagles waived Max Runager after the fourth game of the 1983 season, but re-signed him a month later. Who took his place for that short time?

Q104 Nicknamed "Jet Stream," this player was enshrined into the Arkansas Hall of Fame in 1984. Who was so honored?

Q105 Who did Andre Waters displace at strong safety in 1986, which was Buddy Ryan's first training camp?

Q106 What New Jersey town do both Kenny Jackson and Alex Wojciechowicz call home?

Q107 In what year did Kenny Jackson retire during spring minicamp so he could spend more time running his restaurant in Camden?

Q108 In 1989 Kenny Jackson played for another team when he joined that club as a Plan B free agent. The next season he came back to Philly. With what team did Jackson play for that single season?

Q109 Which Eagle kicker designed unmanned radar equipment at Hughes Aircraft, where he worked for two years before joining the team in 1984?

Q110 In 1983, Reggie White was one of the four finalists for the Lombardi Award (best college lineman). Who nosed out White for the honor?

Q111 In a "White" sale of sorts, the Eagles purchased the rights to Reggie White from this USFL team. For which club was he playing in 1984 and part of '85?

Q112 Reggie White was one of two players selected unanimously to the Pro Bowl following the 1988 season. Who else was so honored?

Q113 Free agent Jairo Penaranda hailed from Colombia. What unique childhood hobby led to the development of his toughness?

Q114 Randall Cunningham has gained more career rushing yards than 36 of the 37 running backs selected in the 1985 draft. Who is the only back ahead of Cunningham?

Q115 What was noteworthy about the 1989 Pro Bowl, the game in which Randall Cunningham was the NFC's starting quarterback?

Q116 How many consecutive starts did Randall Cunningham have under his belt before he was lost for the 1991 season because of the serious knee injury he suffered in the first game?

PHILADELPHIA EAGLES

A103   Tom Skladany

A104   Roy Green

A105   Ray Ellis

A106   South River

A107   1988

A108   Houston Oilers

A109   Mike Horan

A110   Dean Steinkuhler (Nebraska)

A111   Memphis Showboats

A112   Mike Singletary

A113   He used to bronco-bust llamas.

A114   Herschel Walker

A115   He and AFC QB Warren Moon were the first black signal callers to start in a Pro Bowl game.

A116   62

*** FAST FACTS ***

With the Eagles' championship shutout wins of 7–0 over the Cardinals in 1948 and 14–0 against the L.A. Rams the following year, the Birds became the first club in NFL history to wrest two consecutive league titles by whitewashes.

The 1991 draft was a banner one for the Eagles, as seven of the team's choices made the team.

CONCRETE CHARLEY:
Chuck Bednarik played in 253 of a possible 256 games with the Eagles during his brilliant 14-year career. Two of the three games he missed were in 1949, his rookie season.

In 18 NFL seasons (1957–63, Eagles; 1964–74, Redskins), Sonny Jurgensen played on only eight teams with a better-than-.500 record.

Q117   Who laid the hit on Randall Cunningham that put him out of action?

Q118   Which Eagle defensive end scored a short-yardage TD as a tailback in the 1986 Japan Bowl?

Q119   Which Bird was a Babe Ruth League teammate of Michael Jordan in their hometown of Wilmington, N.C.?

Q120   Keith Byars ended up second in the 1984 balloting for the Heisman Trophy, despite the fact that he led the nation in rushing, scoring, and all-purpose yards. Who edged out Byars for the award?

Q121   Strange but true: This defensive All-Star was waived on the final cut in his rookie season, 1986. Name the player who came back to prove the coaches wrong.

Q122   In 1991, Eric Allen recorded five interceptions. What was unusual about each of the corner's picks?

Q123   Which Eagle served as a bodyguard for boxer Aaron Pryor in 1984?

Q124   Who is the only tight end to have more receptions than Keith Jackson in his first three NFL seasons?

Q125   On September 24, 1992, U.S. District Court Judge David Doty ruled in favor of Keith Jackson and three other NFL holdouts in their antitrust trial. Who were those three players?

Q126   Which Eagle worked as a sports anchor for WTSP-TV in Tampa in 1988?

Q127   On what type of scholarship did Rich Miano enter the University of Hawaii?

Q128   Which two Eagle quarterbacks played on the same San Diego Charger team for the entire 1989 season?

Q129   This Bird was the first unanimous All-America selection in Arizona State history when he recorded 19 sacks as a senior. Who made his mark as a sackmaster?

Q130   Who has the distinction of being the highest-ranked Canadian ever selected in the NFL draft?

Q131   Keith Byars was the only NFL player in 1990 to throw and catch a touchdown pass in the same game. Against what team did he achieve that feat?

PHILADELPHIA EAGLES

A117 Bryce Paup

A118 Jerome Brown
(The East team's running backs were all injured.)

A119 Clyde Simmons

A120 Doug Flutie

A121 Seth Joyner

A122 Each of the thefts occurred on the road.

A123 Kevin Allen

A124 Kellen Winslow (202 to 194)

A125 D. J. Dozier
Webster Slaughter
Garin Veris

A126 Ron Heller

A127 Diving (He made the football team as a walk-on.)

A128 Jim McMahon
David Archer

A129 Al Harris

A130 Mike Schad (The Rams chose the Queen's University graduate in the first round of the 1986 draft.)

A131 Green Bay Packers

Q1. Which Eagle coach played pro football in Canton, Ohio, under an assumed name?

Q21. What was the name of the Fordham line on which Alex Wojciechowicz first gained fame as a center?

Q157. What did the Eagles do to pay tribute to Jerome Brown after his untimely death?

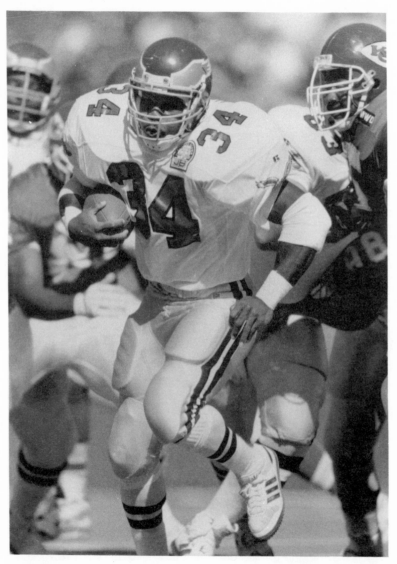

Q149. With what ballet company did Herschel Walker dance?

Q132 Whose streak of 309 consecutive pass attempts without an interception was shattered by Ben Smith in Game 10 of the 1991 season?

Q133 Whose record for career pass efficiency did Jim McMahon surpass at BYU?

Q134 What position did Jim McMahon initially play at Brigham Young?

Q135 Jim McMahon was the fifth overall pick in the 1982 draft and the second quarterback selected in the top five. What QB was chosen ahead of McMahon?

Q136 In the off-season, this Eagle keeps busy in Tinsel Town: He serves as an assistant strength coach at UCLA and has acted in *First & Ten* and *The Last Boy Scout.* Who is this actor-athlete?

Q137 Who was the only rookie free agent to make the team in 1991?

Q138 Identify the six quarterbacks who were on the 1991 Eagle roster.

Q139 Name the Eagle signal caller who quarterbacked the Sacramento Surge to the World League championship in 1992 and garnered MVP honors in the process.

Q140 Identify the Eagle who was born in Koiaumi Gumma Ken, Japan.

Q141 Jeff Kemp started his NFL career in 1981; Philadelphia is the QB's fourth team. With what other clubs did the Dartmouth grad play?

Q142 With a degree in art, this Eagle put his education to good use: His work has been published in several books and he is the creator of a comic book called "Ultimate Man." Who is this artistic grid star?

Q143 Roy Green was a fourth-round pick of the Cardinals in 1979. What position was he initially going to play when he came to the NFL?

Q144 Roy Green was one of three NFC receivers to lead the conference in receptions in 1983. Name the two other "colorful" pass catchers.

Q145 This Eagle, whose father played 11 years for the Lions, was the only Notre Dame player to see action in every game during his four years with the Irish (1987–90). Who is he?

Q146 In 1985, in the USFL, Herschel Walker set a pro football single-season rushing mark with 2,411 yards. How many 100-yard rushing games did Walker rack up that season?

PHILADELPHIA EAGLES

A132 Bernie Kosar's

A133 Danny White's (McMahon: 156.9; White: 148.9)

A134 Punter

A135 Art Schlicter (by the Baltimore Colts)

A136 Ken Rose

A137 Brad Goebel

A138 David Archer
Jeff Kemp
Randall Cunningham
Jim McMahon
Brad Goebel
Pat Ryan

A139 David Archer

A140 Guy Bingham

A141 Rams (1981–85)
49ers (1986)
Seahawks (1987–91)

A142 Mike Flores

A143 Defensive back

A144 Charley Brown
Ernest Gray
(Each caught 78 passes that year.)

A145 Scott Kowalkowski

A146 He had 14, including 11 in a row.

THE UNIFORMS

Q147 Herschel Walker began the 1992 season by rushing for 114 yards against the New Orleans Saints. When was the last time an Eagle broke the century mark in rushing in an opening game?

Q148 A change of scenery appeared to be just what the doctor ordered for Herschel Walker. He racked up 1,070 yards in his first season—1992—in an Eagle uniform. How many other 1,000-yard seasons had Herschel achieved in his NFL career before he accomplished the feat with the Birds?

Q149 With what ballet company did Herschel Walker dance?

Q150 On June 25, 1992, Jerome Brown was killed in a car accident in his hometown of Brooksville, Fla. What other NFL player had lost his life two days before when he was struck by a truck that had veered off the road?

Q151 What did the Eagles do to pay tribute to Jerome Brown after his untimely death?

Q152 Match the Eagle with his retired number.

A—Steve Van Buren	15
B—Pete Retzlaff	40
C—Al Wistert	44
D—Tom Brookshier	60
E—Chuck Bednarik	70

FYI

Q1 How did the Eagles acquire their name?

Q2 The Eagles have had seven home sites since the team was formed in 1933. Name the facilities the Eagles have called home.

Q3 On October 22, 1939, the Eagles made history when they appeared in the first televised pro football game. Which team thumped the Birds, 23–14, in the milestone contest?

Q4 In what year did Art Rooney buy half-interest in the Eagles and the Birds move their home site from Municipal Stadium to Shibe Park?

PHILADELPHIA EAGLES

A147 1934 (Swede Hanson vs. Green Bay)

A148 One (1988: 1,514 yards)

A149 Fort Worth

A150 Eric Andolsek of the Detroit Lions

A151 A patch marked "JB 99" was placed on each player's uniform.

A152 A–15
B–44
C–70
D–40
E–60

A1 The club was named "Eagles" in honor of the symbol of the New Deal and NRA.

A2 Baker Bowl (1933–35)
Temple Stadium (1934–35)
Municipal Stadium (1936–39, '41, '47, '50, '54)
Shibe Park/Connie Mack Stadium (1940, '42, '44, '57)
Forbes Field (1943)
Franklin Field (1958–70)
Vet (1971-present)

A3 Brooklyn Dodgers (at Ebbet's Field)

A4 1940

Q5   Because of a manpower shortage during World War II, the Eagles and Steelers merged for one season, 1943. By what name was the team known?

Q6   Who were the "One Hundred Brothers"?

Q7   The Eagles played their first game at Franklin Field on September 28, 1958. What was noteworthy about the team's debut at that site?

Q8   Why was 1958 called the Eagles' "Year of the Big Triple Play"?

Q9   Despite being trounced by Cleveland (41–24) in the 1960 season opener, the Eagles had a long winning streak in their triumphant campaign. How many consecutive victories did they compile that year?

Q10   To whom did the Eagles dedicate their 1969 season?

Q11   August 16, 1971, marked the first Eagle game at the Vet. Who did the Birds thump 34–28 in the preseason contest?

Q12   In what category did the 1973 Eagles lead the NFL?

Q13   What was the name of the WFIL Radio show hosted by Stan Walters?

Q14   Despite an 11–5 record in 1979, the Eagles lost the Eastern Division title though they were tied with another team. Who took the top by winning the tie-breaker?

Q15   What was the Eagles' record in the strike-shortened 1982 season?

SETTING THE STANDARD

Q1   The Eagles topped the NFL in two offensive categories during the 1990 season. What were they?

Q2   In another testament to the Eagles' defense, only one team gained more than 300 yards against Philadelphia during the 1991 season. Name the opponent who achieved that feat.

PHILADELPHIA EAGLES

A5   "Steagles"

A6   They were a group of Philadelphia businessmen who in 1949 invested $3,000 each to purchase the Eagles from New Yorker Alexis Thompson for $250,000.

A7   Philadelphia was the first pro team permitted to play its regularly scheduled home games at a college stadium.

A8   Buck Shaw replaced Hugh Devore as head coach. General Manager Vince McNally acquired Norm Van Brocklin from the Rams in the team's biggest trade ever. The Eagles switched playing sites from Connie Mack to Franklin Field.

A9   Nine

A10   Astronauts Neil Armstrong, Buzz Aldrin, and Mike Collins, whose lunar module was named "Eagle."

A11   Buffalo Bills

A12   Pass offense

A13   "On the Line"

A14   Dallas Cowboys

A15   3–6

------------------------ . ------------------------

A1   Time of possession
          Rushing yards

A2   Washington Redskins (357 yards)

Q3 The 1991 Eagle defensive squad finished at the top of the NFL heap against the run and pass, and allowed the fewest yards. Sixteen years earlier, another team achieved the same feat. Identify the club.

Q4 At 3.0 yards, the 1991 Eagles set a league record for fewest yards allowed per rushing attempt. Which team's mark did the Birds eclipse by one-tenth of a point?

Q5 For 54 consecutive games, the Eagles did not allow 100 yards rushing, until they ran into a running machine on November 1, 1992. What team broke Philly's impressive streak?

Q6 Chuck Bednarik has the distinction of playing the most seasons in an Eagle uniform (14), but another durable athlete played in more games. Who holds a team record for seeing action in 180 games?

Q7 Harold Carmichael's streak of 162 consecutive games played puts him at the top of the Eagles' list in that category. Who is a close second with 159 straight appearances?

Q8 In his first full season as a starter (1971), this free safety paced the NFL in interceptions with 11. Who made a name for himself with the thefts?

Q9 His 1,965 yards and 25 touchdowns were good enough for this Philly quarterback to lead the league in passing for the 1948 season. Who was this talented signal caller?

Q10 Name the Eagle who led the league with a 158.3 passing rate during the 1990 campaign.

Q11 From 1951–62, Bobby Walton racked up 881 points, good enough for an entry in the team record books. Who is a distant second with 475 points?

Q12 This kicker holds a pair of team records: most lifetime field goals (91) and most points in a season (116, in 1984). Who was the man with the talented toe?

Q13 The year before Philadelphia traded Harold Jackson and a passel of draft choices to the Rams for Roman Gabriel, Jackson led the league in receptions. How many passes did Jackson pull in during the 1972 season?

Q14 In what category did Harold Jackson lead all NFL receivers in 1969?

Q15 With what San Francisco receiver did Pete Pihos share the pass-receiving crown in 1954?

PHILADELPHIA EAGLES

A3   Minnesota Vikings

A4   L.A. Rams (1967)

A5   Dallas Cowboys (Emmitt Smith gained 163 yards on 30 carries.)

A6   Harold Carmichael (1971–83)

A7   Randy Logan (1973–83)

A8   Bill Bradley

A9   Tommy Thompson

A10   Keith Byars (All four of his halfback-option passes resulted in touchdowns.)

A11   Sam Baker

A12   Paul McFadden

A13   62

A14   Yardage (1,116 yards)

A15   Billy Wilson (Each player had 60 catches.)

SETTING THE STANDARD

Q16   Against what opponent in the 1991 campaign did the Eagles establish a team standard with 11 sacks, all courtesy of the defensive line?

Q17   As the 1992 season began, Reggie White had played in 105 games. How many quarterback sacks had the superstar registered in his career?

Q18   Jeff Feagles led the league in 1991 with the greatest number of punts inside the 20-yard line. How many did Feagles boot inside the red zone?

Q19   This Eagle ran away with a November 6, 1966 game against the Cowboys: He ran 93 yards for a TD on a kickoff and 90 yards for a second TD. He became the first player in NFL annals to return two kickoffs for touchdowns in the same game. Who put his name in the record books?

Q20   This Bird was flying high when he became the first rookie in league history to boot two field goals of 50 yards or more in one game. Who had the golden toe?

GLORY DAYS

Q1   On the first play of the 1948 championship game, the Eagles went for broke and completed a 65-yard TD pass, but the score came back due to an offside penalty. Who connected on the nullified play?

Q2   How many field goals were missed during the 1948 "blizzard championship"?

Q3   The Eagles snagged their first NFL championship in 1948. Who did they defeat in a snowstorm at Shibe Park by a 7–0 count?

Q4   Who scored the only touchdown on the snow-covered field at Shibe Park in the 1948 championship?

Q5   First it was snow (1948), then it was rain as a steady downpour created a quagmire for the 1949 NFL championship game. Who did the Eagles shut out 14–0 to capture back-to-back crowns?

Q6   Who scored the deciding points for the Eagles in the 1960 championship game that saw the Birds triumph over the Packers, 17–13?

Q7   In the 1960 championship game against the Packers, Chuck Bednarik made a title-saving tackle on a Green Bay fullback. Who did Bednarik stop at the Eagle 10-yard line with less than a minute to play?

PHILADELPHIA EAGLES

A16   Dallas Cowboys (Eagles 24, Dallas 0)

A17   110 (White is the only player in NFL history with more QB sacks than games played.)

A18   29

A19   Tim Brown (The Eagles won 24–33 at Franklin Field.)

A20   Paul McFadden (November 4, 1984, against Detroit; 52 and 51 yards)

---------------------- . ----------------------

A1   Tommy Thompson to Jack Ferrante

A2   Four (three by Philadelphia and one by Chicago)

A3   Chicago Cardinals

A4   Steve Van Buren (a fourth-quarter run for the five yards)

A5   L.A. Rams

A6   Ted Dean (five-yard rush with 9:39 left in the game)

A7   Jim Taylor

Q8   How many minutes did Chuck Bednarik play when the Eagles won the 1960 championship game against the Packers, 17–13, at Franklin Field?

Q9   Norm Van Brocklin was at the controls when the Eagles won it all against Green Bay in that 1960 title game. What was noteworthy about that contest?

Q10   In order for Philadelphia to be able to make the 1978 playoffs, two teams had to lose on the final Sunday of the regular season. Name the clubs who defied the odds and went down to defeat, opening the door for the Eagles.

Q11   In the Eagles' first playoff appearance since 1960, the team lost a heartbreaker when this Falcon QB threw two TD passes in the last five minutes of the game. Who engineered the comeback in the 1978 wild-card game at Fulton County Stadium?

Q12   The year 1979 was a banner one for the Eagles: Dick Vermeil was voted NFL Coach of the Year, the team compiled an 11–5 record, and the Birds defeated the Bears in a wild-card game. Who stopped Philly's playoff drive in the next round with a 24–17 win?

Q13   What was the Eagles' overall record in 1980, the year they reached the Super Bowl?

Q14   Which two teams did the Eagles trounce in the 1980 postseason to earn a berth against the Raiders in Super Bowl XV?

Q15   Where was Super Bowl XV played?

Q16   Ron Jaworski threw a 40-yard TD pass in the first quarter of the Super Bowl that was nullified by an illegal-motion penalty against the Birds. Who was on the receiving end of what would have been the game-tying score?

Q17   Name the duo who hooked up for the Eagles' only touchdown in Super Bowl XV.

Q18   This player set the tone in the 1981 wild-card game against the Giants when he fumbled two kickoffs in the first quarter. The New Yorkers prevailed for a 27–21 win at the Vet. Which Eagle had butterfingers in that game?

Q19   What was the score in the 1988 divisional playoff game known as the "Fog Bowl"?

PHILADELPHIA EAGLES

A8   58

A9   The Eagles became the only team to beat Vince Lombardi in a championship game during his tenure at Green Bay.

A10   Minnesota Vikings
Green Bay Packers

A11   Steve Bartkowski (Atlanta 14, Philadelphia 13)

A12   Tampa Bay

A13   14–5 (12–4 in the regular season)

A14   Minnesota (31–16)
Dallas (20–7)

A15   Louisiana Superdome (in New Orleans)

A16   Rodney Parker

A17   Ron Jaworski tossed an eight-yard pass to Keith Krepfle in the fourth quarter.

A18   Wally Henry

A19   Chicago won, 20–12

Q20   Choose whether Philly or Chicago won the following categories in the 1988 playoff game called the "Fog Bowl."
  (A) Rushing yards (164 vs. 52)
  (B) Passing yards (407 vs. 185)
  (C) First downs (22 vs. 14)
  (D) Net yards (430 vs. 341)
  (E) Takeaways (4 vs. 3)
  (F) Offensive plays (75 vs. 57)

TRADES, WAIVES, AND ACQUISITIONS

Q1   The Eagles have the distinction of selecting the first player in the first pro draft of collegians (in 1935). The man they chose was also the first Heisman Troophy winner. Who was the man known as "The One-Man Team"?

Q2   What did the Eagles do after they selected the first player ever taken in a NFL draft?

Q3   Identify the Notre Dame All-American whom the Birds traded to the Boston Yanks in exchange for Mike Jarmoluk in 1949.

Q4   Norm Van Brocklin was acquired by the Eagles in a 1958 deal with the Rams. In addition to a first-round draft pick, Philadelphia sent two players to L.A. in the trade. Who was sent packing

Q5   When the Eagles sent Billy Barnes and Bob Freeman to the nation's capital, they received in return Ben Scotti and the man Frank Leahy called the "greatest center to play at Notre Dame in my eleven years." Who did the Birds acquire in the 1962 deal with the Skins?

Q6   How did the Eagles acquire Dave Lloyd in 1963?

Q7   In a two-for-two swap, the Eagles dispatched Sonny Jurgensen and Jimmy Carr to the Redskins. Which tandem came to Philly in the 1964 swap?

Q8   Ollie Matson was obtained by the Birds in exchange for J. D. Smith in another 1964 deal. What other player came to the Eagles from Detroit as part of the Matson deal?

PHILADELPHIA EAGLES

A20   Chicago—A
Philadelphia—B,C,D,E,F

_____ . _____

A1   Jay Berwanger (University of Chicago)

A2   Onwer Bert Bell sold his rights to Chicago. (Berwanger and George Halas could not agree on terms. Berwanger turned his back on pro football and developed a multimillion dollar manufacturing company.)

A3   Frank Tripuka

A4   Jimmy Harris
Buck Lansford

A5   Jim Schrader

A6   Lloyd and Dick Mills were traded to the Birds from Detroit for a passel of draft choices.

A7   Norm Snead
Claude Crabb

A8   Floyd Peters

TRADES, WAIVES, AND ACQUISITIONS

Q9 In a summer of '64 deal, the Eagles dealt Bob Harrison and Clarence Peaks in return for Red Mack and Glenn Glass. With what team were the Birds wheeling and dealing?

Q10 One player was dispatched to the Cowboys for Lynn Hoyem, Sam Baker, and John Meyers in yet another 1964 transaction. Who went to the Lone Star State in that swap?

Q11 Identify the tackle who came to the Eagles after the team shipped Pete Case to the Giants in 1965.

Q12 In a two-for-one deal, this Eagle stalwart was traded to Tinsel Town for Frank Molden and Fred Brown. Who went to L.A. in the 1966 deal?

Q13 This flanker was acquired from the Steelers in 1967 for Earl Gros, Bruce Van Dyke, and a draft pick. Who made the cross-state journey in the deal between Philly and Pittsburgh?

Q14 A draft choice and this quarterback were sent to Chicago in exchange for Mike Ditka when the Eagles and Bears transacted business in 1967. Which field general wound up in the Windy City?

Q15 Identify the defensive back-punt return specialist the Eagles obtained when they dealt Tim Brown to Baltimore in a 1968 trade with the Colts.

Q16 Whom did the Eagles dispatch to the Left Coast so they could acquire Harold Jackson from L.A. in a 1968 deal with the Rams?

Q17 Which quarterback was dealt to the Eagles from the Rams in exchange for Alvin Haymond in a 1969 swap with the L.A. team?

Q18 Safety Joe Scarpati flew the Eagles' coop in 1970 when the Birds shipped him to New Orleans for Norm Davis and another safety. Who came marching into Philly in the deal?

Q19 Whom did the Eagles receive when they traded Norm Snead to the Vikings in 1971?

Q20 The Eagles had two first-round selections in the 1973 draft. Whom did the team choose with the pair of picks?

Q21 In another major trade, in 1973 the Eagles sprang Ernie Calloway and Leroy Keyes from the nest and obtained a veteran defensive end from Kansas City. Who came east in the transaction?

PHILADELPHIA EAGLES

A9   Pittsburgh Steelers

A10   Tommy McDonald

A11   Lane Howell

A12   Maxie Baughan

A13   Gary Ballman

A14   Jack Concannon

A15   Alvin Haymond

A16   Izzy Lang

A17   Billy Guy Anderson

A18   Bo Burris

A19   Steve Smith

A20   Charley Young
Jerry Sisemore

A21   Gerry Philbin

TRADES, WAIVES, AND ACQUISITIONS

Q22   L.A. unloaded four-time Ram MVP Roman Gabriel in a trade with Philly for Harold Carmichael, Tony Baker, and a slew of draft choices. When did the blockbuster deal occur?

Q23   What did the Eagles give up to acquire Bill Bergey from Cincinnati in a 1974 trade with the Bengals?

Q24   The half brother of the Skins' Charley Taylor, this defensive end came to the Eagles from the Browns in 1974 in exchange for Ben Hawkins. Who was he?

Q25   The Eagles sent John Reaves and a draft choice to the Bengals in the summer of 1975. In return, the club acquired Wayne Clark and this All-Pro. Name him.

Q26   Cornerback Joe Lavender (and three draft choices) were shipped to the Redskins so the Birds could obtain a defensive standout in return. Who joined the Eagles' D in the 1976 trade with Washington?

Q27   How was Ron Jaworksi obtained by the Eagles?

Q28   In what round was Youngstown State's Paul McFadden selected in the 1984 draft?

Q29   Who came to Philly when the team sent Wilbert Montgomery to Detroit in 1985?

Q30   Who did the Eagles select ahead of Randall Cunningham in the 1985 draft?

Q31   Who did the Birds trade to Cleveland so they could select Seth Joyner in the 1986 draft?

Q32   From what team did the Eagles acquire Matt Cavanaugh in a 1986 draft-day trade for a pair of picks?

Q33   From what AFC team was Mike Golic obtained on waivers in 1987?

Q34   With what team did the Eagles swap draft picks so they could select Sun Devil Eric Allen in the 1988 draft?

Q35   Four—count 'em, four—wideouts were drafted by the Birds in 1990. Identify the quartet.

Q36   Of the group cited above, who set an Eagle record for most touchdowns by a rookie?

PHILADELPHIA EAGLES

A22   1973

A23   Three draft choices (two first and one second)

A24   Joe Jones

A25   Stan Walters

A26   Manny Sistrunk

A27   Jaws was acquired by Philly from the Rams in 1977 in exchange for the rights to Charlie Young.

A28   12th

A29   Garry Cobb

A30   Kevin Allen

A31   Anthony Griggs (Joyner was chosen in the eighth round.)

A32   San Francisco 49ers

A33   Houston Oilers

A34   Tampa Bay (The Eagles traded a second- and fourth-round pick for the Bucs' second-round selection.)

A35   Mike Bellamy (second round)
Calvin Williams (fifth round)
Fred Barnett (third round)
Tyrone Watson (11th round)

A36   Calvin Williams (9)